Kelly,
We love you! Thank you for all of your support. You are the best ♡ Kerri

Becoming *Love*

This Book is Dedicated to

Troy William Biddle

Thank you for saving my life
and for teaching me the awesome power of self-love.

Let every day of my life be a reflection of you.

And to

Mark D. Smith

Without whom this book would not be possible.

Becoming *Love*

Kerri Perisich

BALBOA PRESS
A DIVISION OF HAY HOUSE

Copyright © 2012 Kerri Perisich

All rights reserved. No part of this book may be used or reproduced by any means, graphic, electronic, or mechanical, including photocopying, recording, taping or by any information storage retrieval system without the written permission of the publisher except in the case of brief quotations embodied in critical articles and reviews.

ISBN: 978-1-4525-6075-5 (sc)
ISBN: 978-1-4525-6076-2 (e)
ISBN: 978-1-4525-6077-9 (hc)

Library of Congress Control Number: 2012919281

Balboa Press books may be ordered through booksellers or by contacting:

Balboa Press
A Division of Hay House
1663 Liberty Drive
Bloomington, IN 47403
www.balboapress.com
1-(877) 407-4847

Because of the dynamic nature of the Internet, any web addresses or links contained in this book may have changed since publication and may no longer be valid. The views expressed in this work are solely those of the author and do not necessarily reflect the views of the publisher, and the publisher hereby disclaims any responsibility for them.

The author of this book does not dispense medical advice or prescribe the use of any technique as a form of treatment for physical, emotional, or medical problems without the advice of a physician, either directly or indirectly. The intent of the author is only to offer information of a general nature to help you in your quest for emotional and spiritual well-being. In the event you use any of the information in this book for yourself, which is your constitutional right, the author and the publisher assume no responsibility for your actions.

Any people depicted in stock imagery provided by Thinkstock are models, and such images are being used for illustrative purposes only.
Certain stock imagery © Thinkstock.

Printed in the United States of America

Balboa Press rev. date: 1/10/2013

Introduction

The answer is not in any book. You will not find what you seek by looking to a particular exercise program or any one spiritual practice. You can never find peace, happiness, sexiness, or freedom in anything outside yourself. The answers are always entirely within. A book like this is merely a pointer to the key that belongs to you. Open the doors to your own dreams. How could anyone know what is best for you without walking in your own spiritual shoes? I will point you in the right direction and perhaps even influence to take steps to heal and improve your life condition, but you must determine and follow your own course of action. We have all been pointed in the right direction throughout our lives, but never did we get anywhere without giving our consent.

You've got to fill your own soul. You must respond to your soul's inner wishes and longings. Your soul speaks to you in whispers but will shout at you when you ignore yourself for long enough. Guilt and addictions are no more than signposts, shouts from the soul, to point us away from the wrong roads that sap our power. We must listen to what our soul tells us without beating ourselves up for needing a reminder. Hearing the soul is healing; wallowing in what we hear is negative judgment. We must abandon judgment and stick to the quiet teachings of the soul.

The soul speaks but not in words. You can show your soul that you understand what it wishes to show you, but you cannot use words. Talk to your soul with symbols. Let your soul know symbolically that you are ready to let go of the addictions and other negative influences both in and around you that keep you from your true path.

How will you know what to let go of and when? We hold on to so much that we allow our past to define our present and future. We become riddled with past mistakes and the wrongs we've inflicted on ourselves and other. Holding on to such negativity locks us into depression. Worrying over whether our past will become our future locks us into patterns of anxiety. Neither the depression over yesterday nor the anxiety over tomorrow will benefit our living today. The saying goes, "If you keep one foot in the past and one in the future, then you are shitting on today." Simply put, you remain frozen and your present moment suffers. You become incapable of enjoying the now because you've froze yourself in time to continue replaying the grudges from your past or in anticipation of tomorrow's worries and failures.

Many of us hope to numb the ill feelings of today by self-medicating. Nobody enjoys feeling less than great. Numbing the pain keeps us frozen in time as well. The downside to remaining stuck is that the rest of the world continues on with life. When we momentarily step out of our frozen state and look around we realize that we are further back in time than ever.

Addictions provide a temporarily numbing way of remaining frozen in time. Addictions enable us to escape the present moment for any number of reasons. We may feel the now is too painful or boring. Addictions may carry a genetic component, but everyone who has an addiction for whatever reason wants to escape their life because it seems like a nightmare. Addictions gradually destroy our life, creating even more of a nightmare after each use than before we engaged in it. While frozen, we cannot get a sense for the destruction we wreak on the here and now. The victims of our addictions often include others outside ourselves. Our loved ones pay the price for our temporary escapes. We operate today as if it were yesterday while our yesterdays become weeks, months, and years. Operating today as if it were yesterday is a dangerous and self-destructive habit. Would you drive to work with the same attitude on a sunny day as you would in the middle of a snowstorm? Of course not. Yet somehow it has become socially comfortable to remain depressed over depressing events in the past despite changing present conditions. Animals do not operate in this way. They don't hold grudges against members of their own kind. They would never survive if they feared leaving their nest because the world might gobble them up. If animals operated as many frightened humans do, they would quickly become an endangered or even extinct species. But just because we've made it convenient to remain paralyzed with the fears of the past and the worries of the future, it is not okay!

Look within. Look to yourself for the comfort that you're afraid the world can never give you. In fact, the world will never give you the comfort you need. Not right away and not every day. Giving yourself true love is the only way to create the possibility that the world will be able to show love back to you. All the rest of your inner work becomes an active process of letting go so that your inner light can shine even more brightly.

Following our inner sense of self is more than just a good habit to get into; it is everything. It is the key to self-respect, self-mastery, inner peace and authentic happiness. It is so important that if we work on nothing else other than self-love, success and happiness will follow. When we align with our best self, life flows effortlessly through and around us. We gain easy access to creativity and abundance. We spontaneously find the right words and actions emanating from the heart center.

You cannot honor your sense of self if you remain depressed, angry or resentful at the past. Breaking away from such negative emotions is an active process of healing and change. Are you holding on to these negative things and blocking the good from flowing into your life? If so, why?

Chapter 1

My Story

A Lesson in Loss

Troy--my more-than-a-mentor, the man who had saved me from my self-loathing and encouraged me to quit the behaviors that would have brought by destruction--was dead. I found myself crying out, "Oh where did my teacher go?" "You do not understand the world of pain you have left me in." "You cannot understand how alone I feel." When he died, I was surrounded by people but still felt utterly alone in the world. My inner beauty, the beauty that he taught me to find, seemed to vanish when he left this world. I called out in anger, "Why did you even let me find this inner beauty if it could disappear so suddenly?" My only goal had been to be my truest self, and I failed at even the simplest of tasks. *You have not failed*, his encouragement would come back to me. "Then why do I feel like such a failure? Why is every day now full of actions I don't wish for? Why do I feel exhausted and unfulfilled?" I lost the inner bliss I had known, like she was always two steps ahead or behind me, hiding in the forest, hurrying from tree to tree. I caught glimpses, but I never caught her. At least not at first.

The first month was full of false promise. I really thought I would be able handle my daily life because I could still feel his spirit all around me. When I saw his body at the funeral I became so filled with his presence, it was as if every particle that had made up his living being was still with me. It wasn't until after 40 days that I felt his spirit leave the earth. Only then did a deep and indescribably painful feeling of loss begin to drag me down. The pain wouldn't leave me for even a second. I could be laughing on the outside, but I was always crying on the inside. I lost pleasure in every activity I once enjoyed. People occasionally invited me to activities, but I found it as difficult to say "no" as "yes." Just trying to form simple words demanded tremendous effort.

My mind played tricks on me. I could no longer intuit anything from my scrambled emotions other than despair. I felt as though everything that had been fun about my life--being free, having fun, and feeling sexy--drifted away from me one grief-stricken day at a time. The spiral took me ever downward for the first two years. I couldn't sleep well, yet everything in my body wanted to crawl into bed and stay there until the nightmare was over.

I knew that getting out and exercising would help me, so I tried it. My old exercise routine became just a whisper in the past. I only barely attempted a bike ride before I stopped and fell asleep on the nearest park bench. It hit me that this was much more than an emotional and a mental tragedy. Every day became an uphill battle. Just getting out of bed felt impossible on some mornings. At one point I convinced myself I had only 30 days left to live and started figuring out who should take custody of my daughter in the event of my death.

Beyond becoming a physical, emotional, and mental train wreck, I lost faith in myself and in my ability to live out my dreams. Without my beloved mentor, I lost sight of the point of living. The thought of worldly success seemed empty and shallow. I had plunged into despair in every possible way. I knew I wanted to live, but I felt sentenced to a life of hopeless nothingness.

Two years passed and I still derived no enjoyment from life. Every coping mechanism left me just as empty as before. I turned to sugar and caffeine to pull me through every weary day. I justified this behavior by telling myself that at least it was better for me than alcohol or drugs.

By year three I felt freed from the fear of impending death around every corner. I even experienced five minutes of real hope here and there. I fooled myself into thinking I was doing better than I really was. I had graduated from heavy despair to moderate depression, but I was far from healed. Without that spiritual coach in my life to tell me how great I was doing, it was as if two people really died that day. The authentic person I once was died with him. I was living for others because I had no clue how to get back in touch with my lost inner voice and intuitive sense.

Graduate school seemed to darken the last light that had shone inside me. I had to exhaust every bit of my energy just to pull through. I wanted great grades, and I took my teachers, clients, family and friends before myself every step of the way. After all, I did not want to face up to how intensely I had been ignoring myself over the past few years.

By year four I began to accept that I would spend the rest of my life living for others. I felt empty and out of control, bound by my addiction to sugar and caffeine. By year five I had left graduate school with my Masters, but I had a weight gain of more than 60 pounds. I decided that I had to put a stop to living for others. It was no easy turnaround. I left my counseling job which had been rewarding but ultimately far too taxing on my body and spirit. I gave up coffee. Not being a cold turkey person, this process took more than six months to complete. I added daily exercise, a routine I had stuck to for so long but abandoned when I began abandoning myself. Quitting sugar was the hardest step and required the most help. I added supplements to fight against my digestive system's buildup of candida yeast, and I called a dear friend every day to track my progress in kicking my addictive habits.

Eventually I started writing again. I was able to do this only after reestablishing my sense of personal power. I began to truly believe in myself without having to lean on anyone else. I got my life back. I got Kerri back, and she was more than worth fighting for. You also are worth fighting for. Never give up on yourself!

Aligning with Spirit

How can you catch your best self when it seems to have run off? I thought I had lost myself for good, but my great loss taught me an even greater lesson: We all must stop feeling like lost souls and take immediate responsibility for discovering ourselves anew.

Healing and aligning our lives with the guidance of Spirit is an active process. We hear the old adage, "Time heals all wounds." Maybe, but time has a way of retaining all wounds until we deal with them by bringing them to the surface. Just as we focus on physical healing when we injury our bodies, we must play an active role in our spiritual healing process. You are not going to be accidentally healed without effort on your part. The only times I've heard of instantaneous healing is through divine intervention or near-death experiences that border on the miraculous. Miracles await us every day, but if we wait passively for them we will never experience their healing power. Rather than wait around for lightning to strike, strike out on your own and take part in your own healing process!

All your actions are worth questioning. One step to the left or to the right in the wrong direction can end up costing you dearly. To avoid your missteps snowballing into disaster, get into the habit of self-examination and make objective improvements to get your life back on the right track. Practicing self-observation is like watching yourself from afar, as if you are just an observer noticing the details of your own life. Pay attention to yourself. It is amazing how little attention we pay to ourselves as we zoom through this life, falsely believing that we need to attract attention from outside ourselves. Vernon Howard, in *Mystic Path to Cosmic Power*, states that self-observation is your very best tool for spiritual growth. Counselors often model self-observation to their clients, reflecting back what they see as objective observers. From the position of self-observer, we are able to see ourselves in a whole new way and with a nonjudgmental perspective. Self-observation is a means to coming in closer contact with ourselves without diving so far into ourselves that we risk self-pity and hopeless despair.

Mindfulness also serves as a mode for self-observation, bringing us out of ourselves. The more we ground ourselves with an objective eye, the more naturally we will take the right action. Our power of spirit rises and speaks to us more clearly when we pay attention to ourselves with a clear focus, so clear that responding to our spirit becomes spontaneous and even effortless. As Deepak Chopra's fourth law of spiritual success teaches, by doing less we end up accomplishing more. Self-observation and mindfulness to our inner spirit become the modes by which we can act with great simplicity and tap into an even greater source of personal power.

Observing ourselves also helps us break through patterns of denial. Denial includes all the excuses and justifications we resort to after we've abandoned our true selves. Denial enables our problems to continue. I know of no one who smokes with the hope of getting cancer, or drinks and drives with the desire to kill other drivers. Yet these results are predictable consequences of such behaviors, and denial that encourages their abuse. To break the chains of denial's repetitions, do nothing more than simply and objectively observe yourself from a distance. When we watch family and friends in action, it is easy to see what they are doing wrong and what they can do to change their lives for the better. The problem is that it doesn't matter how many other people outside of you can see it; it matters only that the person who needs it the most can see it. It matters only that you see you.

If you want to see reality for what it really is, you must observe it objectively. And just as obvious as watching your friends' and family members' lives, you will be able to see the areas in your life that need changing. You will see your life as clearly as an outsider looking in. You will still have your personal denials, but they will gradually lessen as you take action to bring the denials out of the darkness and grow your spirit in the light of objective truth.

As you watch yourself, become aware of any goodness you might be preventing from getting in. Just as forest critters leave tracks and clues to their identities, your life leaves you clues as well. Say for example that you notice yourself watching too much TV. This habit drains you and becomes an energy vampire in the center of your life. Instead of judging your behavior as right or wrong, simply notice your actions. Our bodies are naturally self-correcting when we listen to them. We need only to be made aware of the problem and see it for what it really is. We will naturally gravitate toward the right path when we see the truth of the false path. If we notice that we are "watching TV" our life away, we gain the awareness of what we are missing out on. We begin seeing how the damaging effects of our behaviors far exceed their temporary benefits. Objective observation anticipates outcomes and seeks to avoid potential dangers. By noticing what we don't want, we will more easily spot what we do want. We achieve the rare opportunity to glimpse clearly into the direct consequences of our own actions and the results of our behavior as they emerge.

Transformation Through Spirit: A Lifetime of Work for a Moment of Change

When it comes to change on the level of spirit, too many of us expect a lightning rod of awareness to strike so everything in our world suddenly becomes different, new and somehow better. However, change does not come this way most of the time. Rarely does lightning strike and correct the mistakes of the past, crystallizing a perfect future in an instant of light. Those who do testify to experiencing such an enlightening epiphany seek its illumination for years, so it only seems like a sudden moment. More accurately, the process of deep change comes to us through spirit like fumbling through a game of Battleship. We cannot see the workings of our inner healing mechanisms just as we are blind to our opponent's battleship grid. At first you must make a string of guesses as to what will work. In time you seem to get lucky in locating a piece of a long battleship (i.e., you heal a specific place within you that was in pain). When you find this hit, you stay close to that one area until you've exhausted it and healed the entire location. Then, with one area of pain resurrected into wellness, you continue on in your search for other battleships freighted with pain. Once you sink them all, you feel freed from the chains of your past in the blissful liberation of an instant. A drawn-out application of healing techniques triggers a seemingly sudden moment of healing, and you wonder what ever took you so long to realize this moment. It takes time, patience, and self-knowledge to know what you are looking for, but everyone possesses the inalienable right to personal freedom from the chains of the past.

Feelings are the shadows of today's actions. What you feel sticks close beside what you think and how you act. Your feelings can become stuck inside a place of depression and negativity when you allow your thoughts and actions to create an energetic stronghold over your life. This is why fun activities can help to break a depressed mood, if only temporarily. The goal here is to challenge negative behaviors and thought patterns that afflict the emotions. Shifting your thoughts impacts our emotional state.

However, any lasting emotional shift must also happen energetically. The energetic strongholds that control our lives can make change seem impossible, and no lasting change can happen in an instant. It would be like trying to make a full stop and a U-turn after cruising in one direction at top speed. It takes time to slow down before making the dramatic shift away from the negative course. We must shift our lives on an energetic level if we hope to create the change we wish to see. We are in control, in tandem with the healing power of Spirit. We clean up our energetic prisons, one area at a time.

Because there exist four aspects to ourselves--the spirit, mind, body, and emotions--our vision for personal happiness can become murky and forgotten as we try to balance these four aspects. The mind takes the reins from the body, or the emotions drown out the spirit. It can be cripplingly easy to forget our goal to support ourselves through positive thinking when our emotions run amok. This is why it is critical that we focus on one area at a time as we approach personal transformation. Otherwise we are shooting at targets with our eyes closed. Too many desires compete simultaneously for the attention of the body, thoughts, emotions, and spirit. For lasting change to become a reality, we need to focus on one area of growth at a time. Take, for instance, the goal to improve our self-talk. This goal is too general. We need a specific goal to pursue, one that highlights the power of a specific aspect of ourselves. Shift the goal from simply self-talk to increasing the number of affirming thoughts we think on a given day, and we've isolated the goal to one area. This goal now concerns thinking, the realm of the mind. The other three aspects--emotions, spirit, and body--can rally around this goal as the mind pursues its accomplishment.

The emotions can guide the goal of feeling less depressed. To do this, your emotions seek out activities that generate a sense of fun. The body can follow the emotions' lead instead of fighting against it. It is hard to feel depressed when you are doing something you enjoy. Depression stays at home. At the very least it is slow to find you when you're busy following your bliss. This is why counseling offices often provide lists with activities suggestions. Counselors know that depression starts to fade when we get out of our ruts and stop indulging in its negativity. Isolation only increases depression. Once you've challenged your emotions to give up feeling depressed, you can challenge your thoughts. Cognitive-behavioral theory (CBT) fuels many counseling practices. CBT sessions focus on helping clients identify negative thoughts and replace these old patterns with new, empowering thought patterns. Over time, the new thoughts reinforce positive emotions and mood. The different aspects of the self work together to empower the whole person.

Is there a message your spirit is trying to tell you? Can you create meaning from depression? When people are able to find meaning from even the most unbearable of circumstances, bearing the hard times becomes more tolerable. The light justifies and purifies the dark.

Balancing all four of your aspects--addressing the needs of your mind (thoughts), body (actions), emotions, and spirit--breaks even the most stubborn energetic stronghold. You need to feel all four aspects working together if you wish to pull yourself up and out. When my mentor died, I was utterly devastated. All four parts of me we crushed beneath the weight of grief and despair. Without Troy, I gained more than 60 pounds and struggled daily for five years under a heavy lethargy that would not pass. Grief's stronghold over my energy had made a home inside my body. And no matter how intensely I attempted to get well, I could not seem to break free from feeling like my entire energetic power was gone for good. In time I was able to find my way back to pure faith and hope. I remained an emotional train wreck, crying daily and feeling as though my happiness was gone, that my belief in myself was gone. My faith in God's healing was out there, somewhere beyond my grasp, and my body was a wreck. I felt more sluggish than ever. Later my longing to have him back turned to anger and hatred at myself for having been so weak. I wrote out my anger in journals and burned the pages in the fireplace, or I threw them away at church. I found a counselor and a grief support group and got serious about my health. I saw a chiropractor, bought a treadmill and began intense supplement therapy to rebalance my body's pH level. I relearned self-belief and met new mentors who could challenge me. I found ways for all of myself--spirit, body, mind, and emotions--to heal and grow to new depths.

I get it now. It took a long time. It required a great deal of work, but I get it now. If not for Troy's death, I could not be here writing to you in the way that I now understand human suffering and deep healing. I would not so strongly believe that we all can return to a place of peace and love, even when all we once felt was despair, hopelessness, loss and emptiness. There is a way out! There is a way to freedom from the prison of the past. All we need do is fight for our very lives. You are heading into transition. You need to make yourself the one and only priority. You've got to stand up for yourself because no one else will.

Think of just one thing that you'd like to be different in your life. Make that a priority. It is up to you and you alone to create the space you need to grow and blossom into the person you know you are inside: the person you can be. It all begins and ends with you. It may be up to you to take the steps, but there are millions of people out there who feel, think, act, or are impassioned in ways that you feel, think, act, or are impassioned. Connect with them. Find meaning in what you've gone through, and move beyond it. On the other side you will find deep peace and gratitude for the spiritual transformation you've undergone.

Chapter 2

	I CONTROL	I DON'T CONTROL
MY PROBLEM	**1** 40% investment PERSONAL POWER, TO IMPROVE YOUR LIFE SITUATION *"How I treat myself"*	**2** 10% investment EXTERNAL STRESSORS AND CHALLENGES, SET BOUNDARIES AND LET GO TRYING TO CONTROL *"How the world treats me"*
NOT MY PROBLEM	**3** 40% investment YOUR LIFE'S PURPOSE IN THE WORLD, THE LEGACY YOU LEAVE BEHIND *"How I treat the world"*	**4** 10% investment HOW OTHERS TREAT EACH OTHER, DISTRACTIONS THAT CANNOT AFFECT YOU *"How the world treats itself"*

Using the Energetic Management Grid

We spend too much time and energy worrying and allowing our emotional and energetic powers to cram inside areas that we neither control nor influence. A healthy energetic balance means investing 80% of our available energies into Boxes 1 and 3 of the Grid: the areas that we do control. It won't harm you to spend up to 20% in Boxes 2 and 4: the areas you don't control. That's okay as long as you don't find yourself, like many, dwelling inside those Boxes.

Too often we look to reasons that we have no control over to excuse us from doing anything about improving our lives, which we do control. Spirituality is a way to turn over what we don't control so that we can do more about what we do control. Accepting what we don't control takes time and energy. Turning it all over is an actual physical event. Some do this through prayer. Others keep a journal or see a counselor. No matter how you choose to shift your energies from no control to control, remember that it is an active process that demands energetic release and a commitment to rededicate daily your energies to personal power.

You can use the Energetic Management Grid for any life situation. Take, for instance, your relationship with your spouse. Any action you may take becomes a form of energy that belongs to a specific Box inside the Energetic Management Grid.

Box One (Personal Power): *What do you control that is also your problem?* In this example, you control how you communicate with your spouse, your attitudes toward him, and how you will ask for what you want in the relationship. These three factors also directly affect you and deserve far greater investment than Boxes Two and Four.

Box Two (Life's Purpose): *What affects you that is not your problem?* Death, loss, and your spouse's choices and attitudes all affect you while you have no control. And since you can never hope to control these things about your spouse, you waste valuable energy if you find yourself investing more here than in Boxes One and Three.

Box Three (External Stressors): *What do you control that is not your problem?* This is your life's purpose. You control how you contribute to your children's future by role modeling how to interact healthily with your spouse. Being a positive role model helps your child, so it does not directly impact you. Since it is squarely within your power, however, the energies you invest here are far worthier than Boxes Two and Four.

Box Four (Distractions): *What do you not control that is not your problem?* You can't control the relationship troubles of others or how others look upon your relationship. This is purely wasted energy and has no place sucking power from Boxes One and Three.

***

You can break down any life situation into these four Boxes. Using the Grid empowers you to know how to focus your energy and how to redirect it when you notice it being sucked into areas that you have no control over.

We too often feel responsible for matters that we are far from responsible for. This is where the Grid's boundaries come into play. Apply the Grid to matters in your own life and determine for yourself if you're wasting valuable energy. If too much of your energy is being depleted by things that you cannot control, then it will be nobody's fault but your own when you feel unfocused, drained, angry and bitter.

We can work to transform our lives only from those areas where we have control. This is the realm of our Personal Power (Box One) and our Life's Purpose (Box Three). However, when you waste energy on External Stressors (Box Two) and Distractions (Box Four), you become weak and helpless. You feel you have no control over any area of your life because all your energy is seeping through those two Boxes. How would your life change if you spent more energy in Personal Power (Box One) and Life's Purpose (Box Three)? What would you be doing differently today if you focused primarily on what you do control instead of wasting energy fretting over matters you can never hope to control? The time has come to take back your power by focusing and acting on those things in your life which you actually can do something about.

You can have a new life! You can have the life you want or at least one that approaches the life you want. You have way more power over your existence than you may realize, and when you operate from your areas of power you begin manifesting quick and drastic results in your life.

Once you open up to the possibility of this power of you carry within you, it becomes crucial to know what direction to point your life toward. Your inner intuitive voice becomes your compass. This inner voice is, some believe, the very voice of God. This voice provides you with a power beyond measure. If you can do these two things--listen to your inner voice on a consistent basis and invest your inner power to act on your intuition's compass--then you will discover the key to living the energy-filled life of your dreams.

We must develop the habit of hearing and responding to this inner voice without confusing it with distracting emotions and thought patterns. This voice, planted deep within us, runs below the stream of thought and feeling. We tend to ignore its depth, focusing instead on the material world of surface thoughts and emotions. You must dig beneath the surface in order to hear the voice of your real self. This voice is who you are. It is who you are meant to be. Though it is but a whisper in the roaring thunder of the outer world, it is more real than any shout the world can throw at you.

We put our surface selves in such high demand these days. Our cell phones buzz with instant messages and calls that absolutely must be returned immediately. The excessively speedy chatter has hurt our ability to hear and heed our inner voices. Thankfully there is another movement in the worlds--one towards meditation, mindfulness, centering prayer and spiritual yoga. These and similar centering methods help us to hear our inner voice. Spending time in the silence of nature grants you special access to the greatest friend you could ever hope to meet within any social network: your own self!

If you don't spend your time and energy listening to yourself now, your hidden self will come barging through the door later. This often manifests in the form of depression, anxiety, and addictions. We do so much to suppress anything wrong with our lives instead of listening to the messages our inners selves are trying to scream to our outer selves. Our thoughts, emotions and behaviors want to be driven by our inner personal power. You are the driver of your own life as soon as you allow your inner voice to be heard.

Personal Power (Box One) is the crucial energy area you must fill before you can move into total energetic balance. If you have no power in yourself, you will lack the power to follow your life's purpose and to cut away distractions. You will know when your Personal Power (Box One) energy is strong enough because your ability to manage External Stressors (Box Two) and Distractions (Box Four) will greatly improve. The energies that you don't control won't tempt away your energies like they used to. Though you cannot control these areas, you choose how you will respond. You can choose which attitude you will take when life attempts to knock you off balance. Personal Power (Box One) gives you the energy to step over obstacles and follow the right path for you.

Your path, when you follow it with the guidance of your balanced personal power, leads to the discovery of your life's purpose. This is where Life's Purpose (Box Three) opens up its blessings on your life. This is the area that you control but which influences others outside of you. Finding your purpose can pose a great challenge because there is never any generic recipe for it. It is so uniquely yours that no one will ever share it precisely with you. Just as no two snowflakes are exactly alike, life's purposes don't come as twins. We each have our own unique soul and unique abilities. If you don't know what your life's purpose is, it is likely that you haven't built up your personal power enough to see it. When you can stand in your power and not be blown around by the world, then spend some time exploring what your purpose might be. Force yourself to come up with one, no matter how silly it might sound. You may not immediately find it, but you at least need to get into the practice of seeking for it.

Get into the habit of looking within, not without, for answers. In this hasty information age we've accustomed ourselves to looking outside ourselves for solutions. Expect the answers to come from within. Expect at first, however, the solution not to come to you with crystal clarity. Your purpose will unravel over time as you follow its trail. Identify what you can at first. Think of this seeking as excavating a city beneath the earth. You painstakingly dust off one fossil at a time and determine where that piece goes in the bigger picture of the excavation. You add another piece into the puzzle, and then others, until you begin seeing the whole picture becoming gradually clearer. Ask yourself the heavy questions; you will find your answers.

It takes an active process, a concerted effort. It does not happen by accident. Are you headed down a spiral? Reverse it and head up by reaching as powerfully as possible for what you do want. Stand in line for it. Begin to expect its presence in your life. Get excited about it. What you don't want is well behind you. Today is a new day. Start with a clean slate and fill it with everything you want.

I realize this may challenge the self-doubting part of you. I do understand doubt and self-disbelief. I too have taken the downward spiral. It comes too naturally at times. Why do we allow doubt to pull us down? Personal history and training is part of the confusion, as are memes that selfishly invade our brains. However, it really doesn't matter why. It matters only that we stop and reverse the spiral, ensuring that it doesn't affect us anymore. If the house seems a mess, we stop not to ask why. You simply get cleaning. Your life's "why" is the result of mistakes that were under your control (Boxes One and Three) and events that were out of your control (Boxes Two and Four). Knowing why does nothing for you unless you take action. Figure out what you can do differently in the future. Then get doing it!

Start taking back control of your life by cleaning up your personal power energies in Box One. Invest far more of your power here than in the areas that you are powerless over. Create meaning by leaving your thumbprint on the world through your Life's Purpose (Box Three). You can do it! I believe in you. I wouldn't have invested so much of my valuable time writing all this if I didn't believe that you are powerful enough to create a life beyond your wildest imagination.

Accept the Greatness Within

Greatness is standing in your own power, stepping away from surface distractions, and following your life's purpose. Period. Accepting the greatness within you is self-love. Self-hate is denying your inner greatness. As I examined and processed the pains of my past and got on track with my life's purpose to help others in their processes of healing, I found myself journeying from self-hate into the arms of self-love. Accepting the greatness within is the hardest thing we will ever do in this life. It's almost as if there is a conspiracy for self-deprecation. We fear others when they begin expressing their inner greatness because we're so lost to our own power. This is the fear that others around you will feel when you begin expressing your greatness. You become a mirror to their inner drifting, which frightens them according to how lost they've become. My experience with self-loathing and accepting my inner greatness guided my life's purpose to help others find and express their own greatness. By awakening my greatness I discovered that I am a vibrant, sexy human being who cherishes feeling sensual, sexy and free. Though this may scare people or threaten those who are lost to themselves, I have no control over how others will respond to me. In fact, they do not even affect me. Their attitudes are crammed inside Box Four (not my problem; out of my control), and such distractions are of no use to my personal power or life's purpose. Others may try to make me feel small. They may try to shrink me. But if I end up feeling small inside, it is because I said "yes" to their opinions and "no" to my own truth.

Quit making yourself small in order to appease people who will never be satisfied with you anyway. Self-degradation serves no one. In Personal Power dwells your responsibility to love yourself, to embrace and love the greatness within. Through my experience of grief (a Box Two event), I got all turned around. Because I needed others to get through, I thought I had to take them first. This simply was not and is not true. Needing others makes you vulnerable, not victimized. When you lower yourself to please others you make yourself a victim. Move away from victimizing yourself; empower yourself by taking control of Personal Power (Box One) and Life's Purpose (Box Three) and "letting go and letting God" with External Stressors (Box Two) and Distractions (Box Four). If you can't control it, you don't need to worry about it. Besides, you already have your work cut out for you in manifesting your inner greatness. So get going!

You Are What You Think

Box One contains your thoughts and attitudes. What you focus on, you attract more of into your life. If you keep a positive outlook, you will attract good things into your life. If you wear a perpetual frown, the world will provide you with plenty to feel down about. That's just how it is. Your thoughts are mental arms that grasp into the future. Thinking positively ensures that your mental arms cling to the future good, but this is far different from denial. Denial refuses to believe reality when reality disagrees from what we want it to be. Positive thinking is different in that we acknowledge where we exist within reality while we reach for something better.

We have as much control over our thoughts as we do over what we eat. Our thoughts are a choice we make about how we will feed our mind. Thoughts become mental patterns. Patterns become habits, but it is never too late to change this. You must change your thought patterns and habits if you hope to significantly change your life. You can turn thoughts of bitterness and hate into thoughts of love and peace. This power is available to us all. Thoughts illuminate those parts of your life you choose to focus on. The goal is to illuminate the areas you want to see expand instead of focusing on eradicating the bad. This typically only enlarges the negative areas. Use the power of your thoughts like an energetic highlighter. Focus on the aspects of your life you would like to enhance or enlarge. This is what a gratitude journal does. Focusing on and recognizing the good things in life helps you to see that much more good in the world. You expand the good by appreciating it whenever it rolls around.

Unfortunately, the common human brain often does the opposite. Instead of embracing and expanding the good, the mind braces for the worst. We all can try to brace for life's rollercoaster rocks and shocks; when situations tumble down, however, the fall is going to be hard no matter how diligently we've braced for the coming of the bad. We need to toss out the false assumption that if we expect the worst we will somehow be ready for it. No amount of worry will prevent any disaster. By investing your thoughts into avoiding catastrophe, you pretty much guarantee that a catastrophe will strike. The universe responds to how you prioritize your thinking by replicating the content of your thoughts. The real disaster hits when you've spent up all your thoughts on worry and have none left to invest when a real trauma happens to you. You've put all your eggs into the basket of avoiding trauma. This leaves you with nothing when the time comes to take action in the face of crisis. You have no friends or social support because you didn't invest in forging relationships. Where is your connection with your higher power? Where is your inner confidence to respond to the crisis? You are tossed in the wind because all your thoughts--all your energies--were wasted on avoiding the bad that you have nothing left to receive the good when you need it the most.

Where are you investing your thoughts right now? What do you think about? What input do you allow into your mind? Do you help yourself or harm yourself by following your present thought trails? When you begin inputting thoughts that benefit your personal growth, your life brightens without you even having to try. Spend the bulk of your thoughts on attracting what you do want instead of avoiding what you don't want, and the universe will respond by making your journey easier. After all, isn't it easier to swim with the currents than to struggle in vain against their heavy flow? You'll always have life disturbances to deal with in Box Two, and distractions come and go in Box Four, but these become more manageable when you begin thinking with yourself and not against yourself.

When tragedy confronts you in External Stressors (Box Two), you always have the power of deciding how you will respond. When Troy passed away, hopelessness and a lack of self-belief began seizing me. I took up obsessive behaviors. Food and energy drinks became my addictions, my crutches. Everything I did not want in my life suddenly became my life. I tried my best to stay connected with supportive people, but I did this by doing everything I could to please them at my own expense. Since there seemed to be no hope to find my own happiness again, I could at least derive temporary joy from making others happy. Every day my thoughts prioritized for others and against myself.

Seek help if you've fallen into self-destructive thought patterns that you can't seem to snap out of on your own. Make sure your help comes from someone who will not permit your self-destructive patterns to persist without you confronting the cycle and stopping it. Eventually you will come to a place where you can conquer the cycle on your own, but you risk far less by intervening before your thoughts cause serious and lasting damage to your self-esteem and feeling of self-empowerment. Do not attempt to rebuild your life on your own at the very start. The bigger the burden, the more effort is required for one human to carry it on his or her own. That is why the world is full of people. Every person you meet is a potential source of support. Far more than merely a source of socialization, people form a network that can help you through life's ups and downs. Your soul knows everything will be all right when it sees people stepping in to help you along until you are ready to help yourself.

If you are not presently in the midst of trauma or self-destructive thinking, don't forget others who are bankrupt of beneficial thoughts. They wake up without any sense of inner support and their days blaze by without meaning. Never forget them just because you are doing okay. Help someone when they are down and they will never forget it. Think about a time in your life when you were down. Think of how clearly you remember who was good to you and who ignored you. Helping each other is integral to living in a loving and healthy environment. We need each other, and this is okay no matter how individualistic the world becomes. Invest your thoughts into bettering others. They need you, but are you there for them? I often wonder how differently my teen years could have unfolded had a mentor come to improve my life from his abundance of self-love. I can't help but think that someone should have been there for me but chose to remain absent.

Don't underestimate the power of contributing in even small ways to the enrichment of others. A helper would have changed my whole world before my self-loathing got out of hand. Did my helper fail to show up because he was too caught up in his own busywork? Don't fail others by being too busy or by being anything short of who you really are. Invest your thoughts and time in ways that benefit not only you but the world around you as well. The goodness you sow into the world will return to you in so many ways that you can never anticipate. We all are interconnected and are at our cores all part of one greater being. Move beyond judgment and dare to expand yourself by investing your thoughts toward manifesting your truth to the world instead of keeping silent to please others. Protect what goes into and out of your mind. Make sure your thoughts are your own. With an average of 65,000 thoughts passing through the average person on the average day, what are the chances that every thought we think belongs to us?

Examine your thoughts. Is a negative quip really your mother speaking to you through the past? Are the criticisms you feel yourself really the negativity of your enemies, which you've taken for your own truth? If so, challenge these thoughts. You will begin seeing better results over time as you reap the rewards of new and more self-affirming thoughts.

Your thoughts have value. Thoughts are the building blocks of the tangible world. Because we have a seemingly infinite supply of thought particles, which are planted in our minds over time through countless sources in the media and from our social circles, we mistakenly believe our mind is a force unto itself. This is learned powerlessness in action. Examine your thoughts. Examine your beliefs, which are thoughts that have taken root. It is vital to know which thoughts belong to you and which have been planted there by selfish influences outside of you. If you want to truly experience yourself, you must weaken the outer world's influence over you. Practice mindfulness to dial down the world's volume. You cannot approach a complete relationship with an understanding of yourself while remaining susceptible to outside chatter and delusion.

Begin a meditation practice to turn up your inner volume. Your internal voice begins as just a whisper. You must crank it up if you hope to hear its expression in your life. Speak for yourself; don't permit the words of others to speak through you like a ventriloquist's act. The world is a storm of countless thoughts, but it does not have to control you. You need only awaken the genius within. Your inner genius arises once you've switched off the world's noise and influence.

Examine Your Grid

Are your energies healthily balanced or not? Perhaps you invest more energy into what you don't control (Boxes Two and Four) than into what you do control (Boxes One and Three). What, then, can be done about this?

If your energies are poorly scattered, you need to strengthen your boundaries immediately. Use a combination of words, expressions and actions to reclaim your energetic power from people and situations in your life that weaken you.

We should all know how to say "no" to something or someone when we need to. We all should and deserve to know how to walk away from a situation we're done with.

And yet, so many of us remain in environments that weaken us. We do this with a variety of justifications. The overarching reason for staying in any unhealthy and unhappy situation is the inability to see the lines between your life and the rest of the world. We blur the lines especially when we're taught that others' failures are always attributable to our own failings. But this is simply not true. You can hold yourself responsible only for your own faults, and there is no power in boundaries if you focus on everything that falls beyond your realm of control.

The quickest route to learned helplessness is through focusing on what is beyond your control. This sets you up for others to control you. You won't know when or how to say no because you can't see where you end and the other person begins. Boundaries can appear especially vague in an unhealthy environment where certain tyrants refuse to clean up their own garbage, laying it on weaker individuals instead. This can mess your Grid quickly and severely, especially if you were energetically dumped on from an early age. You flail about in any direction, taking little or no consideration for your own power areas. This is how Box Four becomes just an enticing distraction. It takes the focus away from Box One's personal power center and makes the problem seem to disappear. But the problem grows larger: we simply are unable to see its growth. This becomes an efficient mechanism by which we avoid our own life's responsibilities and need for personal growth.

You have got to learn to listen to your inner voice or the blurred boundaries on your Grid will play tug-of-war with your life energy. You must attend more closely to the whisper within you than to the outer shouts barreling at you from every direction. That whisper is you--the indivisible part of your soul afloat on the world's waves of wants, demands, and needs.

When you begin to see yourself as a being of value, it becomes impossible to ignore your voice. Your voice is your very life. Your ability to speak your truth makes the difference between your soul's life and death. Stop ignoring the stillness within and listen to what you have to say to yourself. Your voice of wisdom will reinvest in your life's abundance a hundredfold if you would only stop to hear what she has to say to you.

You need your voice to clarify where you stand in the world. If you are unhappy, your voice will tell you what to do. I listen to her every day. She is my advocate for feeling happy, sexy and free. She guides my life to meaning and purpose. You will not find your voice in any book or atop any mountain or inside any health spa. It must always come from within you because you are the center of your own universe.

Without you on your own side, you become susceptible to the world's ways. The Energetic Grids of others will tug, push and pull you in any and every way. Your energies will deplete because none of your efforts will ever seem to pay off. Investing your power into things you cannot control endlessly exacerbates any temporary pains you may fall into. To heal, you must draw your energetic boundaries and keep to them.

I want you to know that I love you. I want you to know that I feel your pain and hear your story deep within my heart. When I counsel clients, I can sit and listen to their stories all day because their experiences are authentic and real. Even in cases where clients have to be there because they've been court-ordered, they often seize on the opportunity to finally be genuinely heard and understood. I really feel love for you. I care about you. Do you feel alone? It is difficult to let in the idea that a stranger could be sitting here, writing about her love for you. If that is true for you, ask yourself what may be blocking the love from coming in. Do you believe it's possible that you could feel the love?

I love hearing your stories. Time drifts away and sometimes I don't want the sessions to end, especially when the moments are raw and ripe for change. As I child a felt love for everyone--each and every person on the planet. I thought that there was no one "bad person" out there--only people who have been mistreated, misguided, and cast aside. I wanted to go out into the world and love everyone. I imagined a world where I could be safe in showing others love and support. Of course, through the school of hard knocks and my close loved ones' rightful admonitions against trusting strangers, my love for all dissipated. I discovered the world can be harsh, uncaring, unmerciful, and cruel at times. I learned to be hateful, mostly towards myself because I did not want to give up on the human race altogether. After years of internal work and self-reflection I've returned to where I began as a child, that place of unconditional love for all.

It turns out I was right all along. Leave it to a child's mind to understand what it takes a lifetime for adults to grasp. Now that I am older and wiser, I realize it has taken me years to relearn what had come to me so naturally as a child. I do have a deep-seated love for and connection with all of humanity. If I could, I would spend hours listening to each and every one of your stories. We would cry together and laugh together. You see, I feel love for you, genuine love just because you exist in this world. There has yet to be a person I have met that does not fascinate me in some way. We are all of the same divine love within. And I never get tired of seeing or hearing that source within you.

When a person is being true and present to the moment, it is like receiving a gift. This gift is real spiritual power, a gift of seeing you for who you really are in your greatness. Your story is a wonderful gift, one that I could cherish all my life long. All of us deserves that our greatness be cherished in this way.

If there were some way I could reach you, I'd look like a fool. I'd embarrass myself. I'm willing to make an ass of myself for you to know that you are loved. For one, I love you. I don't need to know you personally to know that we are connected. You and I are both an extension of the one source that creates everything. Because of that I can say with confidence that I do love you. I mean what I say, with all my heart and soul. You and I are connected because the same Source flows through us both.

Spiritual, Not Religious

I have never been particularly strong in any one religious faith. I grew up Catholic and bounced through various Protestant churches during adulthood, including Lutheran and Quaker congregations. I've carried out some Buddhist practices, all the while practicing shamanic journeys and medicine wheels to gain insight and wisdom. Though I've felt close with my higher power since the moment that Source spoke to me when I was in treatment as a teen, I've never felt spiritually empowered by church people. I usually rush in, spend my time with God, and am the first to leave after the service. My goal has always been to talk to as few people as I possibly can. I've learned over the years of my experiences that I don't sit like them in church, don't think like them, and don't talk or dress like them. This has left me subject to harsh judgments on more than one occasion. So you can imagine my shock and confusion when God--Great Spirit, my higher power--told me that I was not just writing another self-help book. No. I was writing a book about building your connection to Source, the source of all things. You can call it God. I thought to myself, "This is going to be way bigger than me. Who am I, an average person who still hasn't found her exact church niche, to be writing about God?" God must have some sense of humor! But knowing what I know about getting out of my own way, I've quickly realized that this is not about me, or even for me. This is about stepping outside of myself and allowing the source to come through and touch each and every one of our lives. This book is for you. My hope and prayer is that through this book you may come to know your own higher power as I have come to know, trust and believe in mine. At this same time you will come to know the peace, authenticity and true happiness that come to you when you align with Source. All that you manifest in this life is not of you, but through you. The higher power that enables you is not an outside experience, but one that flows through your being. Westerners might call it having Jesus in your heart. Easterners might call it transcendence. The idea is clear: step aside from trying to control every last aspect of yourself and your world and you will know true power and bliss.

Growing Up

I must begin with the story of a 12-year-old girl whose fear of intimidating men allowed her to be molested. For fear of standing up for myself in any way, I submitted in a night of panic. But the trauma did not end there. The boy who committed the molestation proceeded to brag to his friends about what he had done to me. Those friends told their friends until I quickly became known as the school slut. Coming from a small town, and especially within the small walls of a public school, word travels fast and with fury.

I began suffering the public ridicule in the form of whispered slander. Self-loathing crept in to accompany me through embarrassment and shame. "What is wrong with me?" I closed myself off entirely from any form of love or acceptance anyone might have provided. Barricaded from any good, I projected my peers' negative judgments back onto myself. Convincing myself that I must have been innately flawed, I turned to drugs and alcohol to provide temporary oblivion from the shame. A girl once known as a social butterfly, I became incapable of connecting to anyone. I turned to marijuana because at least with the pot smokers I did not have to spend lunch alone.

Though I was no longer physically alone, the sorts of people I began associating with isolated me spiritually from the greatness I should have known. I ended up befriending the local troublemaker. My parents were waiting for me when I came home drunk. My stepfather called the cops. The troublemaker, my supposed friend, was sent away to juvenile detention for several months. He blamed me for telling on him and his friends, even though they all knew I hadn't ratted them out. Regardless, I was then labeled a nark. Apart from "slut," "nark" is not a label you want to have in the seventh grade. The public shame became simply too much for me to bear. I convinced myself that this shame was justified and that I was innately flawed. I was certain that, at my very core, I was broken. Nobody in their right mind could have ended up in this place of shame and pain without deserving it. Each new day worsened as I withdrew, gained weight, and quit taking care of my self. I felt horribly ashamed and humiliated for even existing. No one needed to punish me; just wearing my scarlet letter was enough punishment for several years to come.

The more I withdrew, the more the world responded by presenting me with people who ignored me. Thus began a vicious cycle of intense self-hatred. Hating yourself is so complicated because there is no escape. Everywhere you go, there you are. It didn't matter if my family loved me. I hated myself so deeply that without knowing it, I prevented even the smallest shred of light to warm my life with its hope. I wanted every day to die. I spent countless hours alone at the beach near my home, crying and trying to find a way to die. The only thing that stopped me from acting on these thoughts was the fear of death itself. Thankfully I had an obsessive fear of death, and I am convinced that I am only alive today because the fear of death overpowered my will to die. No one around me seemed to understand what I was experiencing. If you've never known the cycle of self-hatred and suicidal thoughts, you will have a hard time finding a reference point. But if you have experienced this deep self-hatred and suicidal ideation, you never forget it.

So there I was. I had no one to relate to and was convinced that I was internally flawed, my soul shattered to a million pieces. I was trapped in a cage with myself, who just so happened to want to kill me. The thought was unbearable. How was I to go on? The situation seemed hopeless. When I began gaining weight, I hated myself even more. It was a bona fide nightmare with no way out. Or so I thought.

I was arrested twice for drugs. One of the two times, police officers came to my school and escorted me out during lunch time. Everyone could see what a druggie I had become. "Druggie" was the third label I received, after "slut" and "nark." I didn't even know you could be both a nark and a druggie at the same time. After the arrests I was faced with the choice of either inpatient or outpatient treatment. Since I figured I was eventually going to be forced into inpatient treatment anyway, I chose that right off. I knew heading into it that it meant a three-week wilderness program for troubled teens, and I thought it might be a little like a camping trip. Boy, was I wrong!

Crying in the Wilderness

The wilderness trip took us into the Boise desert, where we were to live off the land for three weeks with a very short supply of rations and no bottled water. We had to boil our own water from the creeks in order to avoid giardiasis, an intestinal bug which some of my peers before me had contracted. In 110-deree weather it can feel like torture to drink filthy warm water. It made me wretch. A handful of flour, raisins and lentils were all we received for food. We were allowed a saltlick, but we had to move the cows out of the way to get at the salt. Not being familiar with cows personally, I did not realize how large they can be. I was terrified when I was alone and met three huge cows coming right at me. They did not fear me at all. Why should they? I was on their turf. Another peer saved me, and I was relieved to find that no one was screaming for their life the way I nearly had. I did not get the saliva-slathered saltlick. I was not ready to share salt with these beautiful beasts, no matter how peaceful they were pretending to be.

Hiking involved a 16-mile march through the scorching weather in search of water. We had to remain fully clothed to prevent sunburns. Hunger was a constant companion, water our daily goal. We had to learn to function as a group and took turns being group leader. Each of us was required to create fire from two sticks with flint and steel before we could graduate the program. Each night we built mousetraps from rocks, sticks and string in the hope (I use the word "hope" loosely here) of catching a mouse to eat. There was not much in the way of food, but one time we did chase a hedgehog for several hours. Catching it was an unrealistic goal, but the chase brought hope to our small band of seven youths and two adults.

Showering was simply nonexistent. My bra was pitch black by the time the trip was over. So much was required of us, including a time of study every weekday. One of the hardest rules for us teens was, "no swearing for one week straight." It was a mind-over-matter trip that required us to push ourselves beyond what we thought our limits were. Those who passed the physical endurance test struggled when it came to the sewing project. Others coped with the lack of food better than others. Still, food remained our favorite topic. Every morning's discussion consisted of what we would order for breakfast when we returned home.

A significant moment for me was when a fellow peer lost her physical endurance test after suffering heatstroke. She was lagging behind. In that environment, friends are as essential as food and water. At one point she slung her arm around my shoulder and I led her to the finish a step at a time. "One foot in front of the other. You can do it! One step at a time." We leaned on each other's remaining mental strength because we had exhausted our physical capacities. Eventually, one step at a time, we made it to the finish and to water.

All of these strenuous exercises and physical challenges would be a self-esteem builder for any teen, but I needed something more before I could really love myself.

A sense of self-love came to me during my three-day solo experience. We called it simply the "solo." Three days completely alone. The rest of the group was nearby (within yelling range), but I could not see them through the trees or hear them because we could not talk. I spent the first day picking berries and enjoying the quiet. The second day a deer and a fawn passed through my camp. This visitation staggered me because I had been feeling so alone. But it was during my third day all alone in the woods that I experienced something truly beyond measure. On that day I felt the touch of God come upon me. It was as though the sun had broken through the clouds to shine down only on me. The feeling was so overwhelming that my knees buckled and I fell to the ground in a tearful reverie. Crying, I realized that God did love me. He loved me enough to come and touch my heart. I knew right then and there that I would never again question my capacity for self-love. Sure enough, to this day, no matter how many bad hair days or embarrassing moments that may come, nothing has ever made me doubt the self-love I feel inside of myself. It was a gift, granted to me by my nameless higher power.

The Power of Giving Thanks

When I returned to the "real world," I was never more grateful for something as simple as a chair. After you've lived off the land for three weeks, you'll express gratitude for anything and everything. All of us in treatment spent most of our waking moments daydreaming about what we would eat when we returned home. Food dominated the nightly conversations, and it all concerned what we would order when we got back. Someone would yell out, "Ham and cheese!" A quick shot of that would spur us on to hike faster and longer than we thought possible.

However, the real gratitude came when everything was given right back to us as quickly as it was taken away. I remember returning to the treatment center feeling immeasurably grateful for, of course, food, water and a shower. But odd things also struck me. I was never more happy in my life to see a chair. After sitting on rocks for three weeks, a chair seemed like the hugest luxury. Chairs are tailor-made to cradle the human behind. They were not designed for dogs or cats or anything else but us. I was so grateful for a chair of my own that I forgot I was still inside a treatment center. I forgot that I was in a meeting I dreaded. Instead, I was completely overwhelmed and in awe that I could sit in a seat designed just for me. The chair was even torn and stained with coffee, but to me it felt like a throne fit for a queen. I was the queen that day, and immensely grateful for something so seemingly small.

It is amazing what gratitude, real gratitude, will do for the human soul. External circumstances needn't change in order for us to access this potential that every one of us has inside. Do not wait for everything to be taken away before expressing gratitude for all you have. You can access your gratitude capacity right now for everything that is already in your life. We sit on a gold mine every day and somehow fail to realize this. The good news is that we don't have to lose it all to find it all. Keep looking for all that you have. You will be amazed at how much you have to be grateful for that you've long been taking for granted.

Keep a gratitude journal. Many recommend and actively use this method. Keeping a gratitude journal keeps us humble. It keeps us in the flow of abundance. It keeps us connected to source and the awesome power of feeling alive. If you feel you have nothing to be grateful for, then be grateful you are not on fire right now. Be grateful that you have at least another five minutes left to live. Start by giving thanks for where you are at, and work your way up.

Be grateful, not proud, of your life's blessings. Pride is the ego's disease. Ego tells us that we deserve everything we get. We worked hard for it, so we are entitled to the world. The challenge to rising on the ego's shooting star is that it must fall. If it is true that we deserve everything that comes into our lives, then life will backfire on us. We run into forces of nature; bad things happen to us, so we must also deserve that, too. Right? The truth is that neither you nor I are masters of the universe. We are creatures of God. We come from a creator far greater than we can imagine, and it is not in our power to keep the world as our treasure box.

We ought to be grateful that the great blessings of creation are so freely given. As Hafiz observes, after all these years, the sun has never once said to the earth, "You owe me." At the same time, I like to think of the earth as saying "thank you" for the sunlight that enables the trees to grow. We thank our creator every time we stop a moment to appreciate what we do have. Giving thanks encourages the blessings to continue flowing. A former boss of mine left sticky notes for me with messages of appreciation for my work. Appreciation is energetic glue, a type of insurance policy that encourages the objects of our appreciation to stick around. I stuck by my boss because her appreciation for me nurtured in me a loyalty to her.

Appreciation is one of the most powerful tools for solidifying

human connection and for attracting more of what we want into our lives, yet it is one of the most under-observed techniques today. Start a gratitude journal today and show appreciation to others. Do not wait for everything to dissipate and then wish you would have appreciated it while you had it. Not everything is given back to you like that coffee-stained chair was given back to me in treatment. Honor what you have and the people in your life while they are with you and you will not dread saying goodbye when the time comes.

In his book *Messages from Water*, Doctor Emoto describes the power of words like "thank you" and "love" in impacting water molecules. Water molecules marked with such positive intentions appeared crystalline and perfect. Gratitude packs spiritual power that radiates through the world of our innermost cells and outward into the world all around us. Own your power of thanksgiving and begin practicing the attitude of gratitude today!

Receive the Miracle

After treatment I learned the power of staying open to receiving the miracles that our creator wants to share. When we close our hearts and shut ourselves off from Source, we limit our ability to experience the miracle. Had my heart been closed to receiving help, I would not have been teachable. Being teachable enabled me to learn the lesson that nature wanted to offer me, the invaluable teaching that I am a child of God. I am lovable and worthy simply for having been born. Being born gives me the right to experience self-love. The love we give to ourselves is an expression of the love that radiates into us from our higher power. Connecting to our higher power enables us to feel our core worth and experience life in a way that being a walking to-do list could never afford.

Connecting to our higher power and strengthening our core spiritual experience gives us the strength and stability we need when the rest of the world marches against us. Spirit and Source ignite within us our buried power and strengthen our life's purpose. The connections you forge with your higher power and with yourself are immeasurably powerful, if you take the time and invest the energy to build those connections.

My Second Spiritual Awakening

Although drug treatment taught me to love myself, it never really taught me how to like myself. Loving yourself and liking yourself are too very different acts. I now loved myself, but I still didn't appreciate my body, my clothes, my hair or my personality. I also continued abusing drugs and alcohol. By my mid-20s my affliction was mostly with alcohol. I would start drinking on Thursday afternoon and not let up until Sunday morning. One time I left the house in the morning to retrieve my vehicle from a friend's house about two miles from my home. To my astonishment I found the car parked in my driveway. Empty Twinkies wrappers littered the floor, evidence of my late night snack on the drunken drive home. I could recall neither having driven home nor having consumed the junk food. My heavy drinking and need for male attention superficially eased the fact that I was headed down a career path that failed to fill my soul. I worked in accounting because it paid the bills and because I was good at it, even though it made me stifle my burning need for social connection and a greater life purpose.

In the middle of all this superficial partying and self-distraction I met Troy, my mentor and great friend. We spent nights out on the Lummi Indian Reservation in northern Washington state, where we stared up at the stars and just existed together. Breathing, relaxing. My problems slowly began disappearing as I let go of the rest of the world and truly relaxed for the first time in the life of my soul.

Letting go of the rest of the world while I listened to music on the car radio that filled me brought me the golden opportunity to distance myself from work, to stop living as a walking to-do list, and to stop feeling badly about all the stuff I "should be" doing. True freedom is when we really soak in and enjoy the moment as it is, without resisting it or judging it for what we think it ought to be.

Many nights we drifted away from the physical world and merged with the unseen dimension of the soul. How would you like all of your problems to melt away right now? You can make almost every problem disappear when you remove yourself from the demands of the seen world and permit yourself to become truly merged with nature's invisible, silent perfection. It is from the place of letting go that we find real solutions and begin to balance our inner and outer life experiences.

This is when I learned how to fly. "Lie back and listen to the guitar," Troy told me. "Let the music take you away." I closed my eyes, listened, and sure enough I did float away into other worlds, new lands. I feared landing the first time because I thought I would crash into an object on the ground. It took effort to really let go and trust the process. Like many, I had trusted only in drugs and alcohol to achieve the experience of letting go, but letting go begins within and needs no outside influences. Once I truly let go without the need for external substances, I really flew. One time I even saw Troy's soul fly out from his body and float towards me. This was all beyond what I thought was possible, but what surprised me the most was the peace that washed over me when I permitted myself to let go of the day-to-day demands of the earth and really set my soul free to fly.

So many nights I returned home from work to find the house shut up, lit only with the flickering of many candles. Nurturing music played on the stereo or from his guitar. All of the day's stressors melted away. I could walk through the door and feel safe, free and truly home immediately. If you do not feel peaceful and relaxed at home, it is time to take responsibility for your own soul health. Your soul needs time to be the priority. A soul alive with the music of its own expression reinvigorates the body in a way that no outside influence on earth could ever do. We need time to experience an environment that supports and nurtures our own soul. It was through this deep peace of soul that I began feeling free to express the feelings that hid within me. One of those feelings was the ability to express my womanhood, the complete expression of my sexuality without feeling hindered by any limitations or doubts over what I should look like or what I should do. Without qualifications and judgments to strip away my beauty, I danced and felt the sexual energy rise from within me, extending out into the safe environment that cradled my inner beauty.

Troy introduced me to the idea of totally eliminating self-judgment and judgment of others. During this time of releasing earthly limitations, the emphasis was always on feeling. Feel yourself. Feel the energy you would like to feel. Give yourself time to feel what you are on the inside. Then move and act upon what you feel. Once you free yourself from self-judgment, begin trusting in yourself. Get to know yourself by giving yourself the opportunity to feel who you are, maybe for the first time in a very long while.

Once I freed myself from the shackles of self-judgment and awoke to the power of my inner beauty, I realized there is simply no sensation more freeing than a free soul. At the very least, your soul needs time to play every day.

Chapter 3

Meeting Your Personal Power

Personal Power Means Accepting Your Inner Greatness

Accepting your own greatness is the hardest thing you will ever do in this lifetime, and it also happens to be your most important task. Marianne Williamson puts it like this: "Our deepest fear is not that we are inadequate. Our deepest fear is that we are powerful beyond measure." We are taught and come to accept that greatness is a privilege reserved for the talented, the famous, and the born lucky. Nothing could be farther from the truth. Greatness lives in each and every one of us. You are beautiful, unique, special, and talented in your own way. Your gifts are unlike what anyone else has to offer. Quite frankly it is selfish of you to continue withholding your gifts from the people who need them. For example, my teen years were particularly troubled. I spent most of my adolescence and early adulthood feeling extremely suicidal, resorting to drugs to make the pain go away. Not until I completed an intensive three-week wilderness training as part of drug rehabilitation program did I first learn how to love myself and embrace my inner greatness. And that was only the beginning of my journey.

Learn to love yourself today. How many lives would we touch if we broke through the fear and simply lived our own dreams, empowering others to do the same? If we feared not to become our greatest selves, how deeply would we inspire others? How might we serve? Becoming who we're meant to be is in fact an act of deep selflessness, a gift we give not only to ourselves but also to the world.

When we approach life and others from a place of genuine inner authenticity, the juggling act of serving the self and serving others comes into balance naturally and with perfect ease. Like a mother with her children, when we take care of ourselves we have more energy to invest into others. This involves not only our levels of physical energy but our spiritual reserves as well. When we take care of our souls by staying true to our inner nature, we naturally become better able to nurture the souls of others. If nothing else, we can at least serve as an inspiration to others.

How can you take the steps necessary to awakening your inner power and authenticity? You need an inner reference point to refer back to. Call it your intuition or your inner guidance system. We all have an intuitive center despite our efforts to live outside ourselves. All paths return us to our inner intuition, which is where we become who we are really meant to be. The problem with living outside ourselves and looking to others for deep inner guidance is that very few if any people will truly know you or support you on your inner journey. If they already did you wouldn't need to read this book on finding your inner greatness, would you? The good news is that it takes only one person to change your whole life. One person can believe in you with enough depth of belief to wash away all your self-doubt. That person, of course, is you! Be your biggest supporter. Lavish yourself with unconditional positive regard. This means seeing yourself in the best possible light at all times. Hold a positive attitude and be gentle with yourself. Many times we become our biggest enemies when we ought to be our most impassioned fans. I'm here to encourage you to start rooting for yourself and never quit.

Inner Spring Cleaning

If you've got garbage inside you that clouds your emotions and your vision, then it is high time to clean up and meet your best self within. If you take nothing else away from this book, get this: Loving yourself is a must. Loving yourself is a conscious choice that requires time and effort, but go easy on yourself as you undertake this journey. Many times, no one is harder on you than you, so remember to cheer yourself on.

No matter who you are and what you've done, you are worthy of love. Move away from self-hatred. Resolve your pent-up issues. Seek counseling. Keep a journal of your thoughts and feelings. Talk to a supportive friend. How do we resolve the years of junk inside of us? We must let go of the past, including both the bad and good things we cling to. Wishing and longing for what used to be will do you no good. Cleaning the skeletons from our inner closet is essential to becoming our true selves. How can we do this? We begin much like we clean a house. You clean your home one room or section at a time. This can be a long haul if we have little experience with inner spring cleaning. If we can't make the time, then we must take the time to explore what goes on within us. How do we feel? What do we think, and what is the source of our thoughts? Do our thoughts help or hurt us? If we find ourselves hurting on the inside, we must find the origin of this pain and hurt. Rarely does inner pain just shoot up out of nowhere, especially during adulthood. We've got to find the source in our past of the dirt and garbage that mucks up our present. We need to seek out the pain's source, find it, and then remove it.

Let's say you feel angry because you feel someone is not taking you seriously at work. Ask yourself when you have felt ignored or not taken seriously in the past. Perhaps you felt ridiculed in the past when you told your father you wished to become an artist. That past feeling of ridicule colors your actions and feelings in the present. Take time to honor these old feelings, but in the end release them. Much like we peruse through old boxes of junk before we toss them out, we first examine our old inner garbage before ridding ourselves of it.

To release emotions that have built up over time we must step up and step out of them. This is a proactive process of healing and personal discovery. Imagine sitting in a thick swamp of sticky mud and muck that you want to escape from. You need a rope or vine to pull you out, otherwise you remain in your pile of inner garbage, frustrated at your feelings and thoughts that keep you stuck. The vine that brings release has a name: Gratitude.

There are two types of people in this world. There are those who receive $100 every day for five years and when the gifts quit coming, they are pissed off. Then there are those who are thankful for the five years of gifts. I am grateful for the time and the gifts that this life has brought me. Each moment is a precious present. We are blessed with the gift of life and the consciousness of life. Every day we spend with one another is not assumed or expected. Some of us will not get a next day or even a next second. Appreciate your days while you have them. No one of us is guaranteed a future, so none of us are in a position to take anything for granted. Appreciating what we have helps us cope in the face of less. Being grateful for what we had fills us with empowering appreciation. When we only notice what was taken from us, we become empty and bitter inside.

The way up and out, once we've identified the content from the past we are now ready to release, is to follow along the path of gratitude and appreciation. We can access gratitude for even the most horrible experiences. Perhaps we can be grateful for the tragedy simply because we lived through it, that we are still alive. We can even express gratitude for seemingly simple things, like a sunny day, as long as we do so with depth and sincerity. Everyone's object of gratitude will differ, but the purpose of the act remains the same. Gratitude is the vine to which we can cling to pull ourselves up and out of the inner mud. No one wants to remain in the filthy pity swamp forever. You do have the power to bring yourself out of much of your own negativity. The wisdom of gratitude is a power we all carry inside us.

Laughter, along with grateful appreciation, is good medicine. It is also a lot of fun. We are meant to have fun in this life. Tlingit Natives are always cracking jokes. We laugh at ourselves and retell stories we've all already heard just to keep the laughter fresh. Shift your focus from what you lack to what you have in spades. Appreciate life's shifts, and bubble up with gracious laughter.

Many of us, myself included, can ignore the fact that the work begins and ends with us. If we want out of our inner swamps, we must do the heavy lifting. We must express gratitude and thus free ourselves from bondage. If you wish to be happy within, then you are the one who must do the work. Besides, if you look to others to do your work, you likely will find them wallowing in their own self-created stews. You, I, and everyone could easily justify remaining hurt and angry for life because of the rape, tragedy, murder, betrayal, and destruction in the world today. Though we could justify remaining stuck, we will never arrive at healing and wholeness until we stop looking for justification and start seeking to rectify ourselves. I imagine you picked up this book, flipped through the pages thus far, and are feeling that you want something more in your life. I suspect you've grown tired of feeling less than your best self. Don't get stuck with these feelings. Though you may be right in expressing your miseries to the world, the goal of inner spring cleaning is to experience the pain and then let it go. Letting go does not make you wrong or weak. Letting go makes you free. We need to free ourselves from all past experiences so we can come to the place where real creation happens. If we continue feeling the pains and even the joys of yesterday, then we are not ready to actively participate in today. Permit the past to bubble to the surface, to the here and now.

The past wants to be felt and then freed. All too often the past tries escaping into the present moment, only for us to repress it because we don't like its timing, or we do not care to feel the pains of yesterday creeping into today. However, acknowledging the past is the first step toward freeing yourself from it. Some experiences will take more time to release than others will. Some experiences will never fully dissipate, so we must learn to live with them. We do our best to create meaning with the scars that remain after the release, to add purpose to our lives in the face of heartbreak and loss.

We most certainly do not wish to live in the past all the time, but many of us do. We feel yesterday today and have not yet released it, responding as if the same day keeps recurring on an infinite loop. When we connect the dots from today's feelings to their origin in the past, we approach the issue's core. We release the deep wounds inside that block healing. The deeper the wound, the deeper must the healing penetrate. At the surface, we may believe we are angry with others simply because they are all jerks. My boss is a tyrant, my spouse is immature, or the other driver in traffic is irresponsible. We point outside ourselves to explain our internal angry feelings. To be angry at someone for cutting you off in traffic may be a common reaction, but it is not conducive to living as your best self. Your best self cannot feel normal if you stay angry at the world. Anger signals us that something is wrong inside. We look for clues outside of us. We notice the person cutting us off and, voila, there is the reason for our anger. But if the other driver could actually plant anger inside you, then every person ought to react angrily at being cut off. But of course some drivers simply shrug it off and drive on. A discourteous driver cannot spoil a person's day without their consent.

We are, at our core, peace. But we muck up that peace with trash and filth. In an unnatural state vexed with anger and rage, we will curse at the wrongs of others. If it is your normal to react with anger the instant anyone wrongs you in any way, notice this about yourself and understand that a source dwells beneath your reaction that can explain your surface rage.

With my clients, especially the children, I describe the anger volcano. Anger in this illustration is the secondary emotion, spurred by the primary emotion running underground beneath the volcano's surface. The primary emotions tied to anger include fear, abandonment, rejection, and personal violation. The explosive behavior and rage is merely these primary emotions exploding up from beneath the surface. Too often we clean up the lava above the surface but continue ignoring its deeper cause. If we address the cause in our work to clean ourselves up inside, we can prevent future explosions from happening.

One way to dig deeper to the core of your surface frustrations is by asking yourself to identify what lies beneath. For example:

"Who am I mad at?" *My boss.*

"Why?" *Because she chewed me out at work.*

"Why did she do that?" *Because I screwed up a big project.*

"Can I trace my mistake at work any further back into my personal history?" *I guess I've been screwing up ever since I decided not to go back to school for engineering. Now I'm stuck at this crappy job I hate and have no desire to perform well in it.*

"So, who am I really mad at for the situation I'm in?" *Myself, for not following through on my career goals.*

The point here is to go deeper, to search below the surface and find the real root of the problem. Another technique involves asking yourself the five "why's." For example:

"Why am I angry?" *Because my boss is a jerk.*

"Why do I feel like my boss is a jerk?" *Because he refuses to listen to me.*

"Why do I feel upset because he refuses to listen to me?" *Because I feel like he's not the only one not listening to me.*

"Why do I feel like he's not the only one not listening?" *Because I have been burned and abandoned by so many people in the past."*

"Why does being burned in the past make me angry today?" *Because feeling abandonment prevents me from living the life I want to live.*

Notice how the answer to the first "why" question grew far deeper and more personal by the fifth "why." Once you come to a more substantial reason, you come to the core of your present issue. You are well on your way to healing and personal freedom. You are not powerless to a rude boss or to some motorist who cuts you off in traffic. You can deal with the core issue by asserting yourself in a way that meets your realer, deeper needs. Freed from the inner chains that drag down your energetic power, you can put your freed energies to greater use.

If we don't take the time to get beneath the surface, we begin seeing the world through the eyes of hurt, anger, or fear. The world appears to be flawed in the people and situations it presents to us when all along the root of the problem has rested deep within us.

Yet another way to go deeper is by practicing free speech, either with someone else or on your own. Yes, this does require talking to yourself. Contrary to popular belief, self-talk does not make you crazy. In fact, the understandings we reach when we hear our own voice speaking to us can empower us. The key is always to go inward. Both the problem and its solution are found within yourself, not in anyone else or in any situation that surrounds your life. Though you may need others to put your solutions into practice, it is always from within that you will either resonate with the answers or not.

The Empowering Act of Self-Forgiveness

No one will ever be harder on us than ourselves. There is no way to feel self-love while holding ourselves in personal contempt. Instead of loving ourselves into the people we ought to be, we often punish ourselves. All of us have acted in ways that were out of alignment with our best selves. If we were aligned and acting from a place of centeredness, we would have done differently. The challenge is that the guilt we feel over being misaligned only adds to the dilemma. We came upon an obstacle that pulled us away from ourselves, and now our guilt becomes an even more impassable obstacle. If I put up my child for adoption because I cannot afford to raise her, I could choose to label myself a bad person, or I could choose to learn from the pain and look forward to a brighter future. If I receive money or drugs for sex, I call myself a prostitute and bury myself with shame and embarrassment. We attach judgment to ourselves when in reality the feeling is meant to be honored, learned from and then released like any other negative emotion. When we continue owning shame like it is an inextricable part of ourselves, we fall into the syndrome of self-judgment. We judge ourselves, anchoring ourselves to the past.

Why do we become our own obstacles? It seems so destructive, so counterintuitive. Instead of falling victim to our past mistakes and blaming ourselves for our brokenness, we ought to learn from the missteps and move on. My first supervisor gave me a simple teaching tool I like to demonstrate with my counseling clients. The guilt rock. Guilt and shame are natural responses to acting in ways that misalign with ourselves. Instead of projecting the guilt within and living beneath an increasing burden the size of Everest, we carry a small guilt rock with us as a reminder that guilt ought never to become a crippling boulder on our backs. There is no shame in learning from our mistakes and becoming a better person in the process.

It is never too late to be that person you were meant to be inside. We really do get a fresh start every new day. We are capable of great change, regardless of what faulty wiring has previously controlled our brains. We can choose to make better choices and learn from shame without being controlled by it.

Just sit with the negative feeling brought on by your actions. Permit everything to come to the surface like lava. Feelings bubble up and they really do leave the body if you let them. The longer the feeling has stuck with you, the longer it will take for it to leave you. But when it's gone, you'll feel light and relieved. Once you sense that the negative feelings have no further power over you, ask yourself what you learned from the experience. The key here is to learn from your past experiences so that you won't need to make the same mistakes twice. This is the difference between critical self-judgment and useful self-awareness.

Judging yourself harshly is like chaining your feet to the ground. You can never climb the ladder to peace when you stay in self-imposed chains. This takes real emotional and physical action, but you can do it. The process may be difficult, but it is far more crippling to remain chained to judgments. We fool ourselves into thinking that it's the judgment that keeps us from repeating old mistakes. The feelings behind the judgments are the inner compass, our way out. Judgment comes in handy once we climb out of the self-loathing pit. Use it to anchor yourself then, but not while you're still stuck in the mud. An anchor in the mud will only drag you down deeper into despair.

Positive judgments you can use once you've freed yourself from the mud include finding new friends, staying away from the locations that incite your negative behaviors, and using your judgment to determine new and encouraging friends and places you can associate with.

None of us can stay planted in our emotional muck and make it smell pretty. It doesn't work that way. Getting out requires effort and a clear purpose. If I can do it, I know you can. Don't think that just because you're stuck and other people are free that the process is impossible for you. Listen to and learn from others' stories of healing, and always be gentle with yourself through the entire process.

The act of self-forgiveness opens pathways to energetic powers previously unknown to you. To maximize your growth, seek out the following three things:

1. A supporter. This support comes from within. You are your biggest fan!
2. A mentor. Find someone you can speak your truth to. Or you can meet your truth through a spiritual teacher in a book or on tapes.

3. A higher power. For a relationship with the source of creation as you see it.

To stand in your own power and walk in the glory of a higher power seems easy enough, a simple choice. But how many of us sabotage the lives we want and the relationships we love only to regret our actions later? If standing in our power is such a great thing, then why do so many of us find it too difficult to bear? Aligning ourselves with the higher power is our sacred task. With that one thing under control, all other facets of our lives are covered. Relationships fall into place, our job becomes a blessing, over lives overflow with peace.

So, why? Why don't we all act in this way? Simply put, because the world's populace forms a mass that gravitates away from deep peace, toward superficial pleasures. If five million people do a foolish thing and abandon their inner greatness for the surface appearances of the outer world, their actions remain foolish still. It is not enough to simply go along with the world's flow because the majority of the world is gradually destroying itself. It is best to get off the sidewalk when you feel the march of five million coming against you. If you don't step off that path you will be destroyed. This is why internal reflection, meditation and nature retreats become essential. We need to develop a sense of ourselves, our beliefs, our dreams, our desires and our life's purpose.

You can live in this world and still not know yourself truly. It would be a real tragedy to make it to the end of your life without having experienced who you really are. Self-love means experiencing who you really are and ought to be within. Bringing the person on the inside to the outside is the most important thing you will ever do in this lifetime.

Sadly, it is possible to make it through life without ever meeting ourselves because we can borrow so heavily from other people's notions of who they are. We mimic others because that is simpler than being ourselves. We live through others' beliefs and interests, adopting them as if they were our own. We can also suppress who we are through addictive behaviors. We also can reject ourselves by knowing who we are but hiding that from others. Imagine you won the lottery and never redeemed the ticket. Don't rob yourself and others of the greatness that dwells within.

No matter how appealing the world may seem, it is never worth surrendering yourself to play into the status quo. All methods of hiding ourselves are unacceptable. It is not okay to be resolved to constant self-denial and self-protection. The flower that is forever protected and sheltered cannot grow. It does not get the physical sun and light the way the way we deprive ourselves of spiritual light when we either hide from the world or become trampled under its foot.

Overcoming Ego and Maximizing Personal Power Through Intuitive Practice

The biggest antagonist to our true self and our personal power source is the mind and its face, the ego. The ego is the superficial self we present to the world. When the ego takes charge, the outer world has all power over our lives. When the ego takes control, we move into a stage of emergency and must return to Source.

One of the challenges to getting back is that people forget how to trust their inner self. After all, why should they? So few other people in the world look first to the inner self for guidance. Some may laugh at and ridicule people who listen to inner intuition. But your inner life is no joke! It is serious and real. The only joke (and it is a cruel one), is when you end up living your whole life only to then get let in on the secret that you've lived for everyone else when you thought all along that you lived for yourself. Don't become this. Learn to read the subtitles to your soul's language, now!

Change begins and ends with you. It may hurt, but it ought to hurt. Your life passes you by before your eyes, and you are only a passive observer as long as you fail to honor the inner self. Avoiding your inner self, opting instead to elevate the ego above all, is a serious problem.

So big, in fact, that I venture to say that outside of birth and death nothing is more significant in the life of an individual. Nothing. No problem at work, no quarrel at home--nothing compares to this. Get this one thing right and you will amaze yourself at how the answers to your problems have hidden inside you the whole time. What service do you do yourself by getting caught up in a job that drags you away from your authenticity? Why fight against a spouse when you have no idea who you are and what you fight for? What greater problem is there at this moment than to get to know, honor, and love yourself? Get this one right and the real problems and solutions begin to surface.

It is difficult for many of us to listen to our intuition because we do not connect with its words. The connection must be made and practiced with sincerity. Personalization needs to happen. What does the inner world of the intuitive voice mean for me? I co-facilitate a monthly shamanic journey circle where two of us beat drums at a tempo of 180 beats per minute. The journeyers, visitors to the monthly gatherings, lie on the floor and enter an altered state by focusing on the rhythmic drumbeats. The journeys serve to bring the journeyers guidance, wisdom and inner power. During a recent journey I followed a leaf floating gently down a stream. By itself, what does this image mean? Not much. I saw the image during autumn and spent a good deal of time by the river, so it is not surprising that one of those visions of falling leaves would stick with me. But what did the image mean to me, personally and deeply? To me it meant a sense of being supported by water. I felt able to truly relax and let go, knowing that I was totally held up by the water's nurturing power. This led me to feel a sense of security I had not felt in five years, enabling me to feel prepared for what life has in store for me up ahead. Feeling secure and supported was the message I received from the simple vision of a leaf floating downstream. You may receive an entirely different message from the one I saw. The leaf was not the message; it was the way in which I personalized the image to my life.

The meanings you bring to the images and feelings that pass through your daily life will always be the right ones. The problem comes when we refuse to interpret the world we see at all, accepting other people's interpretations as absolute truth. We minimize the messages our intuitions wish to show us, laughing off our incredible ability to create our own realities. An image of a leaf does not innately carry much impact, so how can you learn to take such simple sights with greater seriousness and awareness? The answer, in a word: Practice! After you receive a message and interpret it, spend the next few days with your interpretation planted deep inside your awareness. Do not look for answers to all your life's problems; simply carry the insights in your heart. Notice how keeping your intuitive heart open causes you to feel supported by the universe, powerful even. I know that when my intuition speaks to me through visions as simple as floating leaves I find it easier to relax and let go at levels of deep peace.

We do not need to force our intuition into action; we need merely bring it into our awareness through dedicated practice and allow ourselves to enjoy its wealth of benefits. When we notice the benefits of the intuition, the mind that sees farther than the ego ever could, we notice the abundance of creation flowing through us. Take time to honor the source within by practicing your intuition. Give thanks that this power dwells within, a power that dwarfs even the brightest mind.

Eventually, as our gratitude for the insights grows, we begin looking forward to the next signal or sign. Hopefully we are practiced enough that we approach all these insights with the seriousness they deserve. Our intuitive practice thus builds upon itself. Just as trust grows in a relationship, you begin trusting your inner voice and it becomes that much easier to trust yourself in the future.

Learn and accept that no insight is too small or too silly. It is worth exploring if it has captured your attention in some way. Too many of us have become experts at tuning out our inner world and functioning on autopilot. Our mind and its ego interprets everything the senses perceive according to its own bias, ignoring anything that goes beyond sense. If something catches your attention on an intuitive, gut level, there is a real reason for it. If you find yourself enjoying a particular activity more than others, take notice! We mistakenly assume that whatever we enjoy doing the rest of the world must also love. Even if yours is a popular interest--the aspiration to become a singer, for example--it is significant because it is particular to you. You ought never to slight something you have a deep interest in simply because it is common. You should acknowledge your uniqueness when it comes to the interests that draw themselves to you. Pay attention to the dreams and desires that call to your inner being. Never let the world direct your interests or control the paths you ought to follow. Ask yourself the heavy questions and take yourself seriously the moment your intuitive sense gives you the answer. You are not some common being; you are you. Your intuition speaks with a language as personalized as your thumbprint. The messages that come to you are best interpreted by your own intuition and by no one else because you are the ultimate expert on you. Some people can advise you on certain details, but you are the final judge of where your life is going. Start giving yourself more respect and authority, and start right now. You do not need a doctorate to figure out the direction your life should take. You need only ask, pay attention, and practice deep and unfailing self-belief.

Once you've read your intuitive voice and have begun taking it seriously, your next step is to take action on what you hear. It does you no good to have all the answers, to know exactly who you are inside, and do nothing about it. The messages your intuition picks up are your roadmap, a quiet guide that speaks to you from inside your heart, leading you toward greater spiritual alignment.

After I followed the leaf through my shamanic journey, I spent the next day letting go and embracing my newly rediscovered security. This is the action of intuition. It would have served me little if at all to know intellectually that I was secure without internalizing that awareness. If I remain in my head only, I still feel scared and uneasy. If this the result, then did my intuitive message help me? Not in the slightest. Allow the messages to truly integrate into your life by taking immediate action on them. Take them seriously enough to do something about them.

One of my first shamanic journeys was of a raven that wanted to see the future. I saw the raven fly around the world a few times and enter the future world, but much to my surprise the bird ended up landing on a grave. The vision was so somber that it quickly brought me from excitement to a deep feeling of future fear and seriousness. I had been wide-eyed about my future at that time, had all sorts of exciting dreams and was ready to see great results. Hoping to see something less somber from this vision of the future, I tried pulling the raven from the grave, but it refused to budge. Finally the raven showed a vision of me in graduate school and of my daughter doing well in her life. The raven, still refusing to move, showed me all this from a far off distance as I moved toward the future. When I exited the journey a tear streamed down my face. I held the talking stick in my hand and shared the content of my journey to the group. I returned home, not knowing what the grave in the vision meant. It had a male energy to it, but I couldn't tell if it was of my mentor, Troy, or my brother or my father. At home I shared with Troy just how grateful I was for him being in my life as my mentor, my lover, my friend. I showed him love with such deep conviction in my voice that one would have thought we were sharing our last five minutes together on Earth. Six months later, he passed away.

Now, shamanic journeys are not meant to predict the future, but they are a way into the intuitive inner world where the heart speaks louder than the head. In my previous journeys I had never met a vision as clear or accurate as the raven on the grave. That was a message meant for me to experience at that time, and because I acted on it I was able to have those last five minutes with my mentor which probably would have been impossible without finding that inner insight. By the way, when I had told him of my love with the deepest conviction, his reply was this: "I already know." There are many lessons I gained from this one response. First, we are not fooling anyone. Somewhere in us, others do sense and know the depth of our love. If they pay attention to us, they can feel how we truly feel about them. Secondly, you do not have to wait until a deathbed moment to share with others the sum total of your caring for them. Both of these are lessons I would have missed had I proceeded solely from my head's point of view while denying my heart's language. Your intuitive voice wants and needs to be heard, and you can strengthen its vocabulary as long as you take it seriously and then act on what it tells you.

You are Responsible for You

When you feel comfortable in your personal power, you will reflect your authentic self into the world. You will also make it impossible for you to get away with old habits of self-ignorance. You might have been able to get away with letting go of your own life before you awoke to your power, but once you take back your power you will begin taking stock of your life. You are responsible for you. At no time is this more apparent than when you stand in your power and reflect that power back to the world.

Your old habits will likely bring you shame, but you can do something with this shame. Rather than rue over everything you've done wrong, rub your nose is your mistakes and promise yourself that you will make yourself a better person because of what you've learned. You no longer wait for someone else to come along and rub your nose in your mistakes. You don't need to get caught to get well. Many of us, before awakening to our power, cannot stand the thought of being held accountable for our negative actions because it means experiencing emotional pain. This sort of emotional consequence, however, is given with positive intent. You experience your mistakes in order to help yourself and move forward. We all make mistakes, but we are not defined by what we do wrong. We are defined by what we make right.

When we examine our behaviors, our process of change boils down to two paths: more of yourself, or less of yourself. You either honor who you are inside, thus empowering yourself; or you dishonor who you are inside, thus disempowering yourself. It is really that simple. We tend to overcomplicate matters by expecting the stars to align when we do something good and gunfire to go off then we do something bad. The feedback we receive is more like a gentle breeze that sweeps through your body, insisting that something feels off. Oprah says, "Doubt means don't." Doubt comes in the form of sometimes faint uncertainty. The benefits of hesitating in the face of doubt come later when we feel more aligned with who we truly are. The fireworks of victory won't go off at the moment we act rightly, but the benefits do come with time. Simply move ahead with quiet confidence when an action feels in alignment with your inner self and move gently away when it feels out of alignment with you. This is the entire process of self-guidance through personal power. The struggle and the doubt is part of our self-created human drama, but life is really much simpler than we give it credit for.

I always say that if I make a mistake, I make it from my heart. If I act from my true and aligned inner self, even if I act wrongly, I can live with the consequences and move toward healing. What I cannot live with is totally ignoring myself to become a success in the world's eyes. Such mistakes that are out of alignment with my heart require so much more effort to forgive and to correct. Acting in misalignment is self-betrayal, and your insides will always hold this betrayal against you until you tap into your power and apologize to yourself for straying.

Watch What You Think

Feed yourself what's positive. The thoughts you take in are like your spiritual food. Watch what you think with the same measure of vigilance as you would watch what you eat. Several books already have discussed how you manifest the objects of your thoughts--how what you think determines the content of your reality. You cannot hope to manifest peace and love while thinking hatred and anger. Thoughts are not a force to be fought. They are merely a machine that runs on its own steam, perpetuating today the thought matter of yesterday. This machine may or may not be under your control; it may or may not be moving in the direction you'd like. It has been said that the average person forms 65,000 thoughts each day. What are the chances that all of them are true? What are the chances that all of them belong to you? Much of what you think has nothing to do with creating love and peace in your world. We need to ignore or simply laugh off those thoughts we don't want, which likely were accepted from a source outside of us. Take away the power of the thought machine and refuse to honor what cannot help you.

Most of us give our unmonitored thoughts way too much power over our lives. We never question where they come from or even think we have the power to rid ourselves of them. You might think your thoughts affect you while you are unable to control them (the External Stressors of Box 2 on the Energetic Management Grid), but you do have control over which thoughts you feed yourself and which thoughts you accept from the people and situations around you. If a prowler were to break into your home, you wouldn't accept him and would do everything in your power to rid yourself of him. Why, then, should you be unguarded and trusting with your thoughts? Don't assume that simply because they are in your home, your mind, that they are welcome. You have just as much right to kick out invading thoughts as you would banish a prowler from your home.

And still we don't question if we even believe the thoughts that run through our minds. We instantly accept them as truth, regardless of whether they help or hurt us. Most of us are falling victim to the enemies running amok inside our own heads, and yet we allow our thoughts to beat us up day after day. What have our thoughts done to deserve such a special place of authority over our lives? All they've done is sneak in while our guard was down. We get brainwashed to the lie that we are powerless under them, that we have no control over what we think. Much of coming into our real selves requires the act of realizing what we do have control over while letting go of what we can never hope to control. However, thoughts fall squarely into Personal Power (Box 1 of the Energetic Management Grid). Though they affect us, we do control our thoughts. We have far more control over them than most of us realize. We can laugh at our thoughts. We can even create new thoughts. If you read the words "purple elephant," your mind will create a new thought in a flash. Imagine yourself accomplishing a goal you've longed to accomplish for so long. That, too, creates a new thought, a new and encouraging thought of personal power and success.

Begin by questioning your thoughts and inherited beliefs. Notice if they are thoughts you can support or not. If they are negative or hurtful to yourself or others, then you need to take the power away from these damaging thoughts. You can take their power away by simply observing them from a place of non-judgment through mindfulness, by allowing them to pass gently through you. You can also decrease their power by laughing at the thoughts and by seeing the humor in having invested so much in them.

I once participated in a laughing yoga exercise where we all had to laugh at our credit card statements. I was amazed at the powerful effect that laughter had of taking the power away from a perceived financial dilemma. Kids laugh at other kids on the playground in efforts to take away each other's power. Your thoughts are part of your personal power wiring, and if they are not helping you become more of who you really are, then they are not worth attending to.

Once you have cleansed your thinking, then you'll see clear to dive deeper into the emotional foundations that determine your feelings and general life mood. Before you replace hurtful thoughts with nourishing thoughts, it is impossible to cure your deeper emotional state. Brightened thoughts nurture a brightened emotional core and feed signals to your body that you are heading in the right direction. Your spirit will incite you into action, guiding you eventually to the discovery of your highest life purpose.

Chapter 4

Letting Go

Living in the Now

Every moment is a new beginning if you allow it to be. There is no way to enjoy the present moment while holding on to the baggage of the past. We all need to be whole enough to sense ourselves, and we cannot find this sense of wholeness if we clutter our insides with yesterday's worn-out thoughts and emotions.

Letting go means sending our emotional laundry through the past and then allowing it to just fly away with the wind. Most people don't let go of old fear programming. We figure on the bad experiences repeating themselves indefinitely. We figure that the tighter we hold onto the memories of past traumas, the more we can ensure that nothing bad will ever happen to us again.

It is pure silliness to believe that somehow we can brace ourselves for something terrible and avoid ever being hurt simply by worrying enough in advance. No matter how clearly you see the approaching train wreck, the devastation of the collision remains the same. We cling to the horrible events in our lives so that we won't forget the lesson, but what have we really learned by doing this? Has fretting over what's passed saved you from future pain? Is it even possible to prevent what's coming?

By focusing on avoiding what we don't want, we end up actually attracting it. We miss what we do want. Repetitive fear only keeps the dead weight of the past attached to you. If holding on to the fears of the past ensures only repetitious failure, then letting go of old fears opens you up to expressing your inner greatness. This is your true self: who you were meant to be. In order to make room for embracing your inner greatness you've got to let go of the past, no matter how great its allure may be.

We begin letting go by first identifying the source of a past pain. We examine the root of this old fear or trauma with the help of a counselor, friend, or even by keeping a journal about it. Then we use symbols to let the past go. Symbols are the soul's language. The soul knows what you mean to say when you use symbolic imagery to aid your healing. Writing the name of a person from your past whom you are ready to let go of and then burning up the piece of paper or tossing it into the sea: this is one symbolic act through which we jettison the past.

After Troy died I was terrified that I or someone close to me was going to die any day. Everything I had no control over became totally clear to me also. I felt terrorized and paralyzed by the clutching fear that I controlled nothing in my life. I began writing down all of my fears and throwing the many sheets of paper away at church. Before Troy's death I spent little time in church, but I soon began to attend every week. I got into the habit of releasing all my fears and anxieties to a higher power through the symbolic act of depositing my papers into receptacles at the church.

Don't underestimate the soul's ability to respond to symbolic acts of letting go. I used to carry around jewelry from previous relationships. Troy encouraged me to let go of any connection to these past failures by letting go of the jewelry that had become a symbol of the past. The power behind this symbolic release was immense for my soul. And after letting go of my fears over Troy's death by throwing away my journal pages at church, I noticed the fearful feeling flee for good. Symbolic release heals us of the past and opens us to the neutral perfection of the present moment. All our power and energy flows from the present, but we will never experience any of our power if we tie ourselves up with the knots of the past.

If You Don't Control It, Let It Go

If you died today, the world would go on functioning. Many feel that this is not possible. No way. How could it? The idea that we control the world is just an illusion. After all, what do we really control? Our thoughts, our choices, our attitudes and our bodies. You control only what is yours. If you think you control some other person in the world, that person has merely submitted his or her will to you. Even your children will provide for themselves eventually. They may or may not live to your hoped for standards, and the fact of this surrendered control is enough to make you lose your mind. In fact, many people take anti-anxiety medications because the very thought of letting go can be terrifying. If letting go terrifies you, as it does so many people today, tap into a higher power. Instead of trying to control the small world, allow yourself to be under the power of an infinite source.

Others develop power and trust issues after childhood traumas. A child feels dominated by a scary parent or authority figure and as an adult fears that surrendering control will mean being dominated by others. Whatever the reason, the fact of the matter is that if we don't surrender control in the face of situations that are beyond our power, our mental and emotional health will pay the price. Believing in a power beyond ourselves benefits us by tapping us into the larger whole. Our life doesn't seem to fit compared to the lives of others who seem "better" than us, but we don't fret this when we allow the higher power to carry us and eliminate the perception of differences.

Faith is the language of spirit. It is the act of reaching for and focusing on what we believe and hope for. When we act on faith we break free from the restrictive chains of the earthly senses. We call upon a source greater than ourselves to provide us strength of heart. When we acknowledge the spiritual world by putting our faith into action, we reap the rewards of a soul full of light. A soul full of the source's light is integral to a life of peace, balance, energy and enthusiasm.

According to Maxwell Maltz's *Psychocybernetics*, "Forgiveness is the scalpel that removes emotional scars." I would add "permanently" to this powerful quotation. Just as you must forgive others in order to love them more fully, you must forgive yourself if you hope to experience self-love. Forgiveness is part of letting go of what you can't control, and this especially includes letting go of your own past mistakes. You have to go easy on yourself. The longer your history of hurt, trauma and pain, the gentler you ought to be. If you consider a child who has been abused in any way--physically, emotionally, sexually--how would someone approach this child with efficacy? Would charging at her or overpowering her with criticism work? No abrasive technique will work on someone who can't forgive herself. She will either run away and fall deeper into self-loathing or will submit temporarily until the overpowering force is removed. You and I both know that a forced submission will be only temporary at best. "A man convinced against his will is of the same position still," according to Dale Carnegie. The same goes for how you convince yourself. You will only shift from a stance of self-hatred to self-forgiveness through gentle and persistent effort. Be gentle, loving and supportive with yourself. This kind of softness won't turn you into a marshmallow. Quite the opposite: you will bloom in the way a flower responds to light and water. We need support, care and a gentle hand in order to blossom into our true selves. If we have not found support in the world outside ourselves, then it is up to us to let go of the demanding world and become our own source of support.

To forgive ourselves, we must first identify what we are holding against ourselves. What are the scars that need removing? Just as a doctor examines scars and develops an action plan for their removal, we must do the same with the scars that are left over after years of others pummeling us with abuses. Once we've identified what the scar is and where it is, we can ask ourselves what it will take to remove it from our life's energetic field. Any good doctor will take the path of greatest benefit with the least cost to the patient's wellbeing. So ask yourself, "How can I remove this scar while causing the least amount of disruption to myself and to others?" Sometimes this can be as easy as writing a letter of apology to yourself and then burning it in the fireplace. Burning is a powerful tool for letting go. Fire consumes in a symbolic act that says, "There's no turning back now." What is turned to ashes is gone for good and will never be seen again. Turning our hurt words into ashes permits us to let go of the past's power over us, which makes room for forgiveness.

Other times, the path of least resistance requires a bit more effort than simply burning up our hurt feelings and experiences. We may need to apologize to someone we haven't spoken to in years. We may need to switch jobs or relocate to a new city. Only you will know exactly how much work you will need to undertake in order to feel the freeing power of forgiveness. You are the only expert on you. As much as we'd like to place the responsibility onto others for our own happiness, it falls squarely into our laps to find forgiveness. We can find assistance from a life coach, counselor or other mentor, but it is always up to us to hear our own needs and take action to achieve happiness.

Boundaries

Walk your own path. Though thousands may walk against you, continue forward as your own person. Establishing boundaries is about discovering where you end and others begin. Yet you still have the power to engage with others in community. Community seems easier as children because we come into the world with wide-open, trusting eyes. We believed the world would fill us with its good until a negative experience or two taught us that the world and its inhabitants can be untrustworthy and downright dangerous. However, we grow older and forget to remove the garbage that was dumped into us and which never belonged to us in the first place. Out of our collected problems, pains, longings and fears, how many of them are really our own? Our responsibility remains to protect ourselves from taking in garbage as well as to keep it out. This does not mean that we heave the garbage back at others. That would only violate their right to establish boundaries. No, we offer the garbage back rather than throw it, much as we would return a gift that someone attempts to give: "You can have this back. No, thank you."

It is like magic. Negativity remains outside of us until we permit it across our boundaries. Unless we remove the negativity in the first place, it will remain with us. How, then, do we remove the garbage if we've already accepted it and it's too late to simply hand it back to the giver? We need to explore what is inside. How did the junk get in? Do we really want to eradicate it? Of our daily thoughts, how many of them are negative? How many of those negative thoughts are own? Given that many or most of the negative thoughts that pass through our brains are taken in from outside influences, how can we return our thoughts to the positive once again? We've got to rewire ourselves for happiness. Connect the dots from what makes you happy to the actions you must take to create more of that happiness within. The more dots you connect translates to additional brain wirings for positive thought experiences.

How else can we bring ourselves up? Brain wiring connections are made, unmade, and remade every day, and the media provides perhaps the widest influence on the kind of connections we make for ourselves. Certain products capture us because our brains have been imprinted with a message that such products can improve our quality of life. It is not inherently bad to be influenced by advertising, but you need to remain an active participant in the kinds of information that your brain takes in. Don't passively accept every message that scrolls through your eyes and into your mind. You must proceed with active alertness because, unfortunately, humans are pulled easily to the negative. The media won't show you the beauty of Mother Earth or the simple joys of being alive on this planet. No, you will most often receive exposure to news on the failing economy, murders and related disasters. As a participant on this planet with its negative tendencies, keep your energetic thought boundaries up at all times and you will preserve your inner power when the rest of the world flails at every negative development.

Fear of disappointing others often thwarts our attempts at building boundaries. We do this by failing to see where we are in our life's picture. We worry instead over how others will receive us despite the fact that we have absolutely no control over others' responses. Our job is not to worry about or control others. We can only be respectful and try our best to go through life without stepping over other people's toes. They, as owners of their own energetic grids, have the right to their own feelings. Caring about others' feelings and trying to prevent them from having feelings are two very different things. We can care, to be sure; however, it is totally unacceptable to sell ourselves short in vain attempts to protect others from discomfort.

Boundaries work by identifying what is within our power and then doing something to protect that. Unfortunately, too much pain, unhappiness, and frustration sneaks in from people not maintaining their own power areas. We often permit others to pass through our personal boundaries, allowing their visions to define us. We accept their thoughts as our own, giving in to a life that is less than what we were created for. This creates tension, unhappiness, and even anger within us. The potential for living as our authentic selves exists within each and every one of us. We can cancel out neither ourselves nor the rest of the world as we work to protect the fragile energies that empower our souls.

We need others, plain and simple. We need each other so that we can see inside our own hearts. We need each other to lean on. We need each other so that we may be fed, live and function successfully in the world.

Yet sometimes we pretend that we don't need anyone for anything. Why? It can be humbling to realize that we can't possibly make it on our own. Healing on a personal level involves joining together. Healing involves sharing each other's story. Yet people can drain each other just as often as they can build each other up. This is why many of us quit reaching for help. We believe that help is not there to be given. We teach ourselves to avoid seeking help. This may be especially true for you if you were raised in an abusive household. You hear a hundred reasons why you'll never be successful, reasons for why you're not worth supporting. You can unplug from the negativity, establish a boundary against the harm, and plug into people who can enlighten, support, and even inspire you. Guilt and blame are environmental contagions that limit your growth in spirit. Check yourself if you have been around such contagious people or situations and bleed the negativity out of you.

We will only be continuously beaten down if we allow the beating to happen to us. However, just unplugging from negativity is not enough. We'll still need others to live as our best selves. We strive for human contact and deep connection because at our core we are all one. We need each other for healing to such a degree that we'll plug into even harmful social situations because our need for human connection is so powerful. Better to work with this need than to struggle against it. Purposefully tap into what makes you stronger, not weaker. Be more of your authentic self, not what the world thinks you are. Find your unique gifts by plugging into social support that provides real honor, love, and support. If you cannot find the support outside your door, you can tap into positive support right away with books and audio programs from teachers who encourage and inspire you. Tap into their influence until you grow strong enough and can find social support around you without the risk of losing yourself in the pursuit of others.

One of life's many paradoxes is how we need people while we also need to be alone. If you want to experience some inner peace, you will need to invest time out in nature or spend some time simply by yourself. Peace is already inside of you; your job is to find it. Once you learn to dive beneath the waves on top of your life's surface, you will find a rock solid entity within you that you must meet and forge a connection with. This solid center will seem like a stranger to you at first, but don't give up the search! The deep source of peace is always within, but you will not connect with it while remaining concerned over the happenings on your life's surface. The path demands that you go deeper; go within, especially when it hurts.

We often prefer to busy ourselves with work, play, and the problems belonging to people outside of us. The roles we play--mother, father, son, worker, and so forth--are simply surface manifestations. If we remain connected to only our life roles we lose our ability to swim our peaceful inner depths. From our center we at last tap into ourselves and start gaining control over our own lives. We manifest self-mastery because we are no longer at the whim of temporary circumstances and changes. We are no longer influenced or negatively persuaded by others. When we direct our focus and our energies into those things we do have control over (Personal Power and Life's Purpose) instead of focusing solely on what we can never hope to control (External Stressors and Distractions), true self-empowerment can begin!

Trauma, Support, and Radical Acceptance

After experiencing a great trauma and entering the process of grief and healing, you will feel a great quantity of your vital energy being absorbed into the External Stressors of Box 2. Because you can neither prevent the tragedies nor control how long they will affect you, you must be willing to allow the process to run its course. Feel all the pain without hoping in vain that the past will return. The more we allow the pain to move through us, the sooner it will move out of us. Acceptance is the key. Accept that pain and loss are natural facets of life, but don't let the trauma suck your energy without finding support through the changes.

Seek a support group or connect with a mentor who can relate to your pain. Like the Antarctic penguins, we can circle together, join hands and weather the storm together, being careful that no one gets lost in the blinding storm. When our personal burdens become too great for us only, we need others to help us bear the burden. People with similar life losses know and understand what you are experiencing. Knowing that we are not alone in the depths of our despair helps to pull us through. Because, after all, we are all one. Despair will try to make us believe that we are all alone in the world and that there is no hope. A heart-to-heart connection is the antidote to needling, hope-sucking despair. It takes a village not only to raise a small child but also to raise ourselves from the mud when life seeks to drag us down.

In this highly individualist world we often forget how much we need and count on each other to survive and thrive. A single battery cannot function like two batteries linked together. Human energy works in much the same way, especially during times of devastation. We need each other for emotional recharge, to become balanced, and to lift our burdens when they grow far too heavy for one person to bear alone.

We were born to function together. Support makes the difference between success and failure in countless ways. Think of a time when you felt supported by a friend, mentor, or family member. What did feeling supported do for your soul? Did you feel energetically filled? Lack of support deflates us. It can feel like the whole world stands against us. Even a single person can move us forward if she provides us with enough encouragement and energy. If you lack a positive support network, it is imperative that you find one. Unfortunately, too many of us are born to families that misunderstand us or don't fully encourage us in the ways that we need encouragement. This is why it falls on us to seek out the support we need. If you're still flailing in life without a positive support network, do not put off this vital need any longer. Find one!

Acceptance is the second piece to moving through the currents of pain and loss. Counselors use the term radical acceptance to describe a level of personal acceptance that goes above and beyond the norm. We tend to deny, repress, and ignore reality, adjusting it to fit our own comfort level. However, reality is still reality whether or not we choose to accept it. Twelve Steps programs demonstrate radical acceptance through the serenity prayer: "Lord, grant me the serenity to accept the things I cannot change, the courage to change the things I can, and the wisdom to know the difference." Sometimes we can act like control freaks. I know I can be at times. Accepting what we cannot control can be terrifying. This means we are powerless over the world, over what happens to us and our loved ones. Radical acceptance means trusting in a higher power greater than ourselves to pull us through.

How can we know that a higher power cares for us, or even knows we exist? We have to trust. Building trust in a higher power is no easy task because we cannot rely solely on our five senses to do this. We must respond solely from our heart and accept that we are loved, cared for, and looked out for. Maybe this is easier if you've had a supportive and trauma-free life, but it is certainly not simple for the rest of us who have felt profoundly betrayed by life's heavy blows.

If you want to feel deep peace and lasting healing, there is simply no way to avoid trusting in a power beyond yourself. The main reason is that our idea of control is merely an illusion. We may feel temporarily empowered by assuming we can control every last detail of our lives, but the fact remains that life is ruthlessly uncertain. We could die today or a century from now. By focusing on a power beyond ourselves to guide us through the ups and downs of existence, we can make the most of the time we've been given.

Sioux warrior Crazy Horse was noted for saying, "Today is a good day to die." This quotation, a war cry against the march of ruthless change, demonstrates the kind of radical acceptance you need if you hope to surmount life's immovable obstacles. Far from a death wish,

Crazy's Horse's sentiment expresses deep trust in the Great Spirit. You can say to your higher power, "I trust you so much that if you take my life today I know it is the right day. Your plan is bigger than my mind can see, and I accept the part I play in this world."

Instead of expressing such radical acceptance at devastating situations we cannot hope to control, we invest our worries and fears into the trauma. Death, divorce, the slanders of others--these become our obsessions as we abandon what we do have control over. We have the power to see and to accept the present moment for what it is. When we do this we strengthen our ability to direct our own behaviors, thoughts and feelings. As we come into heightened fellowship with our higher power, we build a relationship of trust and honor while abandoning our false sense of security in attempting to control the world. Illusions, especially the illusion of control, can never offer peace. Illusions are empty. The sooner we realize this, the sooner we can begin filling ourselves with a real power to love ourselves and to impact the lives of others for the best.

Go Within or Go Without

One of life's biggest temptations is to look outside ourselves for the answers that dwell within. Too often do we think, "If only so-and-so hadn't got in my way, or discouraged me…If only my parents had been more supportive, then I could have been great." I have fallen into the trap of looking to others as the source of my own failures, and I've seen my daughter do it. When she was 7, my daughter grew angry at me for her father's death. I became a tangible, externalized target at which she could direct her inner hurt.

Just because the external target is a tangible person or thing, this doesn't justify distracting ourselves from the real origin of our pain. Who was my daughter really mad at? God, life, me? Mostly, she was expressing her rage at the situation of bereavement. Of course it may seem silly, especially for a 7-year-old, to say, "I hate you, situation!" Why does this seem silly, when it really is the situation that we hate? Why do we so often lash out against others at such times? Our society values the material, the concrete, the visible. We focus and emphasize what we can experience through our five senses. Many look for the ultimate external experience that will heal the internal, intangible self, but no act of displacement can change the fact that it was never about other people. We will only continue to fail until we approach the problem in a way that allows us to solve it.

It cannot be overstated how absolutely your problems are never outside or beyond yourself. Your pains stem from within and determine your existence. Eleanor Roosevelt said, "No one can make you feel inferior without your consent." Why is this true? What if they are really mean and antagonistic towards you, then what? You always have the choice, the power to decide whether you will internalize the external hurts that others throw at you. If the negative messages were given to you from a young age, when you were open and receptive to your surroundings, you still have the choice and the power as an adult to reexamine your past and decide whether or not you will hold on to old hurts.

Most problems begin and end within you. Period. If you are unwilling to grasp this concept at least in part, then there is nothing I or any other teacher can do for you. The buck stops with you. You have to take responsibility for your internal state or you will forever remain powerless beneath it. If you will do nothing about your own inner state, then there is no point in reading any words of wisdom. You have to be willing to see how you've contributed to your own mess before you can hope to live your best life or impact the lives of others.

It is far too easy to see other people's problems and flaws. Holding the mirror up to ourselves is the hard thing. The flaws of others are quicker to spot because our eyes are always looking outwards. What I have found, however, is that most of us already know exactly what we need to do but simply don't take ourselves seriously enough to act on it.

The whole goal of finding this inner peace and confidence is to ultimately align ourselves with spirit. When we align with our truest self we feel a connection to source that surpasses physical problems and brings us a sense of deep peace and fulfillment. So, if inner peace and the inner reality of ourselves is the highest truth and our greatest goal in life, then how did we get so far off track from who we truly are?

We distract ourselves. From day one, we learn from misaligned adults how to put ourselves out of alignment. Though our innate state is to seek balance, we often abandon nature to replicate the influences we see around us. By abandoning nature we abandon ourselves, which at first has its rewards. It can feel good to conform to what we see around us, but as we mature we collect a whole mountain of projections that we think the world forced upon us. When the pain of conforming to outside influences no longer feels good to us, we blame our parents, siblings, or authority figures who we are sure are responsible for how we feel today. However, the painful realities we experience today are products of the truths we accepted yesterday, and it demands an inner act of examination and surrender to move ahead.

Beyond the distractions and illusions we internalize from an early age, society as a larger force will try to oppose our true natures. It is next to impossible to walk against a march of 5000 people heading in a direction opposite to you. There is power in numbers, and society has great power over any one individual. Society is good at showing you how you should feel and act, but they never have your personal interests at heart. The power of large movements of people has led to important breakthroughs and inventions. The slaves were freed, women earned the right to vote, and the U.S. made it to the moon thanks to unified efforts of large groups of people with the support of society as a whole. Though societies can effect big things, they cannot see the individual needs of a single person: You! You need a source to nurture your soul; no society, no matter how benevolent or advanced it may be in the eyes of the world, can ever give you want you need to give to yourself. If the society you live in happens to align with who you are at your core, then you can thank your lucky stars. This rarely happens, if ever. The vast majority of us must fight against the current to be who we are meant to be, and many of us simply fall away and never take ourselves seriously because we think it's impossible to win.

Trauma is another force that can lead us away from authenticity. A death in the family or a sudden illness can make our bodies feel as if we've been knocked out of alignment without our consent. When my mentor passed away, I felt as if everything in my environment had been moved two inches to the left while I kept looking for things where they had been. I couldn't learn the new set of rules that the trauma had enforced upon my life. During such times we need people more than ever to help us through the process of healing. No person can face trauma alone and hope to heal deeply and permanently. The cycle of healing often involves helping others to heal. This gives us a pathway and a purpose for our pain--that we may use the bad for good and feel empowered in a time when our lives feel totally out of control.

Sometimes our own burden, especially during trauma, is simply too big for us to bear on our own. It is important to recognize such times and to ask for help. If you are unable or unwilling to seek help because it is not in your personality (you may be accustomed to being the helper), you need to get over this hang-up. Asking for help when you need it is a must not only for your healing but also for your survival as a person. There can be no avoiding this step, no matter how uncomfortable it may be for you. A little discomfort goes a long way toward healing. The responsibility to heal yourself is yours and yours alone. Identify when you've had too much and speak up for help!

Once you've determined how to avoid the negative influences and rid yourself of old hurts you've internalized, the next step is to have the sense to seek out healthy people who can support your true self. For example, when I was bereaved over my mentor's death, I found myself sharing my story of loss with total strangers at a parade. I found this method, not surprisingly, less than helpful. When I attended a grief support group with others who had suffered similar loss, I found much deeper support. We need to make sure we turn to the right resources during our healing process. There are people and groups out there that want to and can help us if we remain open to their support. Instead of feeling victimized because our close friends and family don't understand or support us, we must keep seeking those resources that are a benefit to us. Real help will hardly ever just walk up to your door and come knocking. It might for a very slim few, but most of us have to do the seeking and the knocking. You cannot permit yourself to remain a victim and hope to feel any measure of healing. The victim mentality and the mindset of healing are exact opposites. Playing the victim is a quick way to dodge responsibility for your own pain, but this will never lead you to lasting success. You do nobody, especially yourself, any favors by playing the victim while you withhold your truest gifts from the world. By swindling yourself, you swindle the world.

I realize my style is direct. If you want warm, fuzzy, and soft, then I am not your girl. I do my best to be nice because I know we need to honor our inner selves. *Nice* could take years for the message to get through, and we simply don't have years. We don't know if even tomorrow is guaranteed. The time to wake up to your own soul is right now! There has never been a better time than now. Earth consciousness is changing. Increasingly more people are growing hungrier for spirit fulfillment and deep inner peace. If you refuse to act now, chances are high that you will be left behind. Use to your advantage the momentum of this new movement toward the spiritual dimensions. Connect with a group of people who bring out the best in you and don't tolerate you falling into the trap of blaming external forces. Create a dire sense of urgency for your life and personal fulfillment. Make yourself the priority!

Let's get back to what happens when we step away from who we are. We learn to do this from an early age. At age 10, your parents tell you that wanting to become a movie actor is a silly pipe dream. You look to your school for support only to find your classmates goofing around in drama class. Perhaps they only took the class so they could earn an easy "A." You quickly realize that your dream of acting is far too grandiose, especially for a kid in a small town of just 20,000. With that information, you limit yourself, taking one step from your core and another step toward meaningless activities that are more practical in the eyes of the world. You enroll in a cooking class, superficially content to be doing something the world approves of more than acting. A seemingly insignificant course change in high school affects your choices later in life. You take more steps away from that early dream of becoming an actor, certain that you made the right choice because your actions now align with the world's practicality. But you will always lose whenever you act against the core desires of your being.

With that first step away from yourself, you tell yourself a lie that you believe is the truth. You lie to yourself about your desires, your very identity. By lying to yourself, you misrepresent yourself to others. It can be far more socially acceptable to lie than to tell the truth about yourself, especially when your truth runs counter to societal norms. But still we lie so that we can gain approval and acceptance from others. It takes a far braver person to speak the truth to others and stand confident with the person that dwells within.

It all comes down to this. Do we ignore the gut feelings of sadness and deflation, or do we honor them? If we honor the feelings, we return to alignment with our true selves. For example, the teen in the above illustration could sign up for acting classes the following year and perhaps go on to teach acting as an adult. She could even make it big in the movie industry. She realigned her life with the creative spirit of her soul, even if all she did was sign up for one acting class.

If we neglect honoring our souls in even small ways, if we ignore our inner feelings, we have to suppress ourselves. This is when our lives begin going wrong. You see, in order to suppress who we are inside, we develop a suppressive routine. This routine can go something like this: "I feel sad that I did not take the class, but it's probably just some stupid class anyway." We need to justify our living out of balance. We minimize our misstep and continue to make more of them. Like judgment, justification serves as an anchor. In order to ignore a true feeling, we need a justifying thought to suppress the truth. This is where the danger comes in. It is in this vicious cycle of justifying our repeated missteps that we deviate from the tracks that point to our true selves.

Justifying our own actions in our heads can be as permanent as cementing the reasons, setting them in stone. We instantly close ourselves off from possibility and see only through the lens of self-imposed limitation. For example, if you were to stand in the center of the room and take three steps backwards, you see the room in a different way from where you first stood. Your emotional and spiritual steps backwards paint for you a new worldview through the crutch of justification. You step into a pretend world, one which requires you to sacrifice a part of yourself in order to justify the lies you've told yourself about how you ought to be in the world. At our core none of us are totally acceptable in the world's eyes. It is not acceptable to be an individual with particular needs and interests. As I said before, most of the time our own desires will clash with what others want from us. When this clash occurs we feel pressured to conform to more standard, acceptable behaviors. This is the moment when our outer world becomes more important than our inner reality. Herein lies the source of all our self-created problems and distractions. We take outer experiences more seriously than our inner identities. But if you don't go within, you'll always go without. It is not merely one problem; it is the entire problem of lives lived in vain striving after wind. When we act against our inner selves to accommodate the outer world, we begin living life as a lie. If we later turn around to tell the truth about ourselves, then we once again walk the road of inner authenticity and true happiness. Living the truth brings us far more peace than living the lie. If we continue living the lie, we prevent the world from ever knowing who we really are.

I can hear some of you out there objecting, "But people tell little white lies all the time. Surely there is no harm in that." However, there is great harm in even a small lie about ourselves. Authentic people have no reason to lie. Once you are true to yourself, you will find it much easier over time to stand in your own truth. The truth is simple; lies are complicated and complicating. Kids tell the truth until they are taught to "know better" and to avoid hurting others by masking the truth beneath small lies that grow larger over time. Lying is the source of most of the pain your soul will experience in this lifetime. If your soul cries out for help, determine where you are being dishonest with yourself and where you are being dishonest with others. Make your inner world a priority by telling the truth and you will amaze yourself at how quickly and intensely your life transforms. Your life may even seem to transform overnight, but the alterations will be the product of the many choices you make in standing up for who you really are inside.

All signs point inwards. To honor who you are inside, to be honest with yourself, to live the stuff of your inner dreams. So, if we feel horrible inwardly, our life will be nothing but problematic. We may have ignored our inner selves for so long that we can only barely hear that still voice inside. The good news is that it is never too late to get back on track and begin getting to know yourself. You already have done some inner work in many small ways. Imagine a relationship based on loneliness, a time you were with someone simply because you felt lonely. You finally mounted the courage to honor your insides and end the shallow relationship. Although you may have felt lonelier at first, eventually you felt more whole for making the right decision based on your inner needs. Right? It is never too late to honor yourself.

One way to figure out whether or not you are on track is to follow what I call the Ten Second Rule. When I worked in accounting I sometimes felt little twinges, hinting that my life was a bit out of balance. It was almost unnoticeable because the twinges were so subtle.

I taught myself to take ten seconds to observe my surroundings every time I felt those twinges of imbalance. A ten second timeout, if you will, to observe my career and life direction. Ten seconds to simply slow down and observe my surroundings.

I learned that if I do not take those little breaks that I would surely enough make mistakes that would be harder and require more time to go back and correct later. After ten seconds I found that most of the time the source of the problem would show itself on its own. All I had to do was take a break and give the problem enough space to reveal itself. Most of us develop a habit of ignoring doubt because we know intellectually to rely on our five senses. However, as magicians show us, the five senses can easily be deceived. They can fall victim to slight tricks. Psychology shows us this as well as advertising. We can become primed to respond to advertisements and subconsciously persuaded to act in ways that benefit the advertisers. We are quick to negate our inner experience and intuition because society so heavily favors outer signals and commands. The world values external empiricism at the cost of the inner reality. But we have an entire "second brain" that wants to experience the world even more intensely than our logical brain. The gut houses the bulk of our body's serotonin, the neurotransmitter regulating mood. Learn to value the gut feelings and instincts that arise from the pit of your stomach. Learn that if something comes to your attention in spite of your five senses, there is probably a meaningful message attached. We in America value the loud, the busy, the external. It is no wonder that too many of us are an internal mess. Just because your inner self speaks slowly and quietly does not mean it's somehow less important than the noisy brain and the external content swirling around your head. Don't be quick to negate your inner experience, ignoring and lying to yourself in favor of the outer world. It is not worth it to empty yourself and fill up the world with your lies. Get in the habit of honoring yourself, of going within, no matter how painfully quiet the experience may be. After all, if you neglect to go within, you will go without. The world will be quick to smother you with energetic boulders that seem impossible to break through unless and until you start singing the song of your soul and never let up!

Cutting Through the Darkness; Letting Your Light Shine

Is there anything holding you back from allowing your light to shine? If a block in your Energetic Grid prevents you from letting the greatness into and out of your life, then bring that block to the surface and let it go. It can be as simple as letting go of anything that is less than great and permitting only the great to shine through you. Though the solution may be simple, the act of letting go can be far from easy. But this must be done if your energies are being blocked from manifesting greatness.

Like a canvas under a painting, our greatness is always beneath the surface colors of our life. We need to clear away what crowds the simple perfection under our surface. Whether our canvas is blotted with anger, bitterness, fear, resentment, false pleasures or a false sense of security, we need only wash away the muck to be left bare with the greatness within.

Ways of letting go are essential if we hope to free up our energies. Find a method that works for you. If you are like me, you might find release from angry feelings by battering a worthless piece of furniture with a baseball bat. Let loose the yucky feelings on inanimate objects that won't be offended by your actions. And once you've let loose, let go! Make the decision to strip away the blocks that prevent your greatness from breaking free. It is your responsibility, and you owe it to yourself and to the greatness inside you.

Some might argue that there is no use in letting go because they only keep failing after making the decision to let go. But the decision to let go is not a one-time thing. You are meant to rededicate to your inner greatness over and over again, with every rising of every new sun. You make the commitment to your greatness as natural as breathing or thinking. For example, quitting smoking demands that you decide to quit not once, but sometimes hundreds or even thousands of times. You never quit quitting until being smoke-free becomes as natural as smoking had been. Inner peace, be it a liberation from cigarettes, TV, or something stronger, requires an active decision-making process that goes beyond passive acceptance. The good news is that the work lessens in intensity once you gain a stronghold over it. Just as toning your body requires more effort up until you get into shape, the work becomes easier once you whip your distractions into shape.

The key is to habituate yourself to healthy and authentic living. Otherwise it would be as silly as thinking you can go to the gym once in your life and magically become slim. It sounds like a great deal of work, and it is. You might object, "Just why is it so much work? Isn't there an easier way?"

If you don't clean up your inner dwelling, your spirit, it will remain a filthy wreck that dirties every other part of your life. All areas of your life--physical, social, psychological--take orders from the very core of your being. Your spiritual state determines how you see the world and how you relate to others. Cleaning up your inner mess is your responsibility, to yourself and to others. You owe it to your friends and loved ones to incinerate your garbage and bring your best self to the table of life. You owe it to the world and to yourself to clean up your own mess. You can't do this while continuing to hold on to the past. You ultimately let go by deciding time and time again to be free.

Once you become empty, you are ready to paint the picture of your true self onto the blank canvas. It is not enough to simply let go of the past. You also have to protect yourself from letting in bad as the future approaches. Make a conscious choice to create what you want for your life. What is it that you truly enjoy doing? Find out what sets your soul afire so that you won't need to feel even remotely tempted to return to your former ways.

Shit Happens

Death. Divorce. Trauma. Disasters. Acts of God. These things happen, and when they do they have the power to suck most to all of our energy. Though we ought to invest no more than 10% of our energies into Box Two, when tragedy strikes we find the ratios flying totally out of whack at no fault of our own. Though we don't control the disasters and instances of loss, they do affect us deeply. So what do we do?

We must still process these events, no matter how traumatizing or depressing, or we will never hope to return to ourselves. I return to the story of Troy's death, the instant all my life energy clotted inside Box Two and I withdrew from myself.

I got the call around four in the afternoon on April 8, 2004. Troy's sister-in-law was on the phone with me. I asked how Troy is doing, for he had been visiting with her up north. "Oh, my God," she whispers to her husband, Troy's brother. "She doesn't know." I know something is seriously wrong, but what happened? His brother comes to the phone. "He's gone," was his reply.

Troy was gone. My beloved friend and spiritual mentor. The one person who saw into my very soul when no one else could see the beauty in me. When I was angry and desperate for love, he saw only beauty and the power of my inner sex goddess. How did he ever see me beneath all the surface ugliness and despair? How did he see such beauty under such a mess? I had always told people that the world would be a better place if everyone had a Troy in their pocket. And now he was gone.

The worst part about his departure from this earth was that he took his sight with him. Over time that beautiful sex goddess, brimming with love for herself and others, faded and became a vestige of the past. I grew so crippled beneath the grief of a loss I had no control over. Simple daily functioning became a heavy chore. I sought out sugar, caffeine and painkillers to pull me through the dark, empty days. Time wore on and wore me out. I lost all touch with the fun, carefree girl I had been. Nothing could bring me happiness or even slight joy. He was gone and he took his ability to see my inner beauty. Thus my ability to see myself seemed forever gone. Gone were all those nights under the stars. Gone was the dancing. Gone was my ability to let go and feel safe in the bitter world.

I trudged along, a victim of circumstance. I put myself last time and time again, just as I had done so many years before. I saw myself disappearing and cried over what I saw, but I was clueless as to how I could get my life back. How could I get myself back? I could forget about pursuits as important as my life's purpose and personal power, for nearly 100% of my energy was crammed into areas that I had no control over.

I quit taking care of myself as my addictions to caffeine and sugar worsened. Thankfully a good friend intervened on the painkillers, but I simply escalated my energy drink consumption to provide false motivation. I grew so lethargic under the heaviness of my days that a dirty dish felt like 20 pounds in my hands.

I had always considered myself a tough and independent woman, maybe even a bit of a control freak in some areas. However, none of my prior confidence at all prepared me for the five years of hopeless agony ahead. My grief experience felt like a simultaneous mix of insomnia, a panic attack, depression, and the flu every day for at least two straight years. Somehow, thanks to the help of some trustworthy friends and my new husband I pulled myself through and began to feel my energies shifting into greater balance.

Never had I dreamed that someone who had known herself so well for so many years could fall away from herself with such force. Clearly I had underestimated the power of grief and loss. During the healing process, though, nothing felt even remotely like healing to me. I simply didn't care whether I healed or not. This is a very dangerous place, the most dangerous pit I had ever known in my life. Apathy in the face of insurmountable grief sucks the energy from your true self with the gravity of a black hole. If you feel no desire to pick yourself up when life's shit hits your fan, then you need to pick yourself up out of the darkness and get busy following your life's purpose. This is where Box Three comes in, the focus of the following chapter. When you feel you can shift energies from Box Two into a healthier area, nothing will bring you greater fulfillment than to impact the world with your spiritual and energetic gifts.

Learn to Say Good Bye

We have such a hard time putting up boundaries between what we want and what we don't want--between what we control and what we don't control--because we are too reluctant to say "good bye" to the past for good. I realize that the concept of forever may scare you, so let's get the obvious out of the way right now. We are all going to die one day. I don't know why we don't all acknowledge this today and every day. There's power in acknowledging death because it puts life into deep perspective.

One day you will have to let go of everything. Let this sink in for a moment. You will release all, including your body and your loved ones. You will cease to have a physical experience. Your job will be filled by another. The world will go on without you. Knowing that you must one day let go of your entire life, can you today let go of your past? Can you bid farewell to all those energies that you don't want and that you can't control? Why not let go of all the ugly, unwanted aspects that haunt your life so that you can enjoy the rest of the days you have in this life without feeling the burden of old pains?

Troy taught me how to say good bye for good from the moment we got together. I had the habit of never really letting go of the past. He taught me to let go of even valuable tokens of the past, such as the two diamond rings I owned from previous relationships. As I watched the valuable jewelry swirl down the flushing toilet, I was struck at the power of that moment. It was the very first time I had taken a stand against my past. I spoke against my past, "You do not own me, control me, or influence me in any way!" By choosing to dump the rings instead turning a profit off them at a pawn shop, I broke free of the old and stepped into the new. I would stand in control of my future, not letting my energies dissipate into those areas (Boxes Two and Four) that attempt to sway me from the areas (Boxes One and Three) that I do control.

In that moment of release I realized that every object around us, as Natives have long acknowledged, holds energy and has the power to influence us if we let them. You cannot stand in the power of the present while being held captive by the tokens that surround you, dragging you back into the worn-out past. Learn to say good bye to what is gone, reject the urge to fear what is yet to come, and say hello to what is!

But you may argue that your past is too painful to let go of. Surely no one wants to add pain to their life, so it is no surprise that millions and perhaps even billions of people hold on to the past in a desperate and fearful attempt to avoid the imagined pain of healing. But you will only hurt yourself more if you do this. There can be no real health in refusing to process the past and step into the present's bliss.

Some may hold on to the past and fear saying good bye because they look at the past as their glory days. They liked who they were then, and it's hard for them to imagine that same glory in the present. The good, it seems, is gone for them. If your yesterday was wonderful, then great! But that is no reason to retire from living today. There is much meaning in store for your life no matter how beautiful your past was. It is up to you to make the most of your present moments. Your life's bliss is not a relic of a distant past. Every day contains treasures. If you can't find meaning and purpose inside the Now, then it is time you start looking.

Whether you see your past as horrible or blissful, you are allowing it to define you when you dread stepping out into the present. Although healing takes time and much energy, the result is more than worth the effort. Throw out the physical cues in your environment that thrust you into the past. Smudge your home with incense or light candles to bring in new energy. Cry all night until you can't cry any more. Do whatever it takes to ensure the past won't hijack you from creating the life you want today. In time and with the right amount of effort, you will become lighter and more alive to what's right in front of you.

Growth is painful, especially the kind of growth that transforms us for the best. You have to walk through the fire to reach the other side. Your days of screw-ups become lessons learned once you decide to let go from the deep intent of your heart. These lessons, instead of dragging you down, now transform you with their bitter guidance. Listen to your inner voice by heeding the past rather than fearing it and releasing everything you no longer need. This frees your soul to grab hold of the life that is right and most meaningful to you and you alone.

Chapter 5

Finding and Following Your Life's Purpose

Get out of Your Own Way

What is your life's purpose? If you don't know it, then get busy finding it. Otherwise you will stay stuck in your own head, in your own emotions, and you will never really be anything in the world. True greatness is found not in your ability to improve your own life, but in your ability to improve the lives of others.

    I discovered that my life's purpose is to write this book as a means of teaching others how to balance their energetic powers and awaken their sexual power within. My purpose is a force that burns through my ordinary days, making them extraordinary. My life's purpose demands that I connect others to this burning source of energy I've found within myself. Connecting to your hidden powers and unlocking your own life's purpose will make you an agent of energetic enhancement in the world.

The significance of finding and following your life purpose cannot be overstated. If found and followed, your feelings, thoughts, and actions will align with who you really are. How will you find your purpose? You and only you will know the answer for sure. I can only point out the significance of finding it.

The root of your life's purpose is your intention. What do you wish your intention to be in this life? An intention can be to make the world a better place, or to live with unshakable honesty, or to take care of the planet Earth. My intention is to help people--to assist them through grief and other life struggles, to be with them as they manifest their true selves, to encourage them to express the absoluteness of their inner beauty.

Once you know what your life's purpose will be, you must develop a plan for its manifestation. Your intention is your spiritual memory, a knee-jerk reflex against the world's shocks. It is the one thing that won't let you get away with misguiding yourself for long.

Intention matters more to the soul than physical action. You will remember every good and bad intention that you ever formed. Going back to my example of intending to help others as my life's purpose, I'm left with formulating a plan. The how-to steps bore the spirit world of intention, descending to the physical world of earthly routine. Here is where we must perform a delicate balancing act between the practical demands of earth and the fire of your spirit. Earth asks what your strengths are. Fire seeks to know your passions. The other two energies, water and air, respectively ask you to assess your feelings and your thoughts as you proceed on your journey to manifest your life's purpose. You must balance these four elemental energies--governing the workings of your spirit, body, feelings, and thoughts--if you hope to make anything from your life's purpose.

Ask yourself, "What am I good at? What am I passionate about? What do I feel and think is right?" Life's purpose comes in that little secret package that only you know about. No one else on this planet can tell you what it is. You've got to be able to hear the sound of your very soul. Other people will be able to reflect back to you ideas, inspiration and encouragement, but only you will know when you've embarked on your one true life's purpose.

A life without passion and purpose is not worth living. It is like living through a robotic computer, plugging away at what you think you are supposed to be doing but really just shifting figures from one point to another. Life without purpose renders you aimless and susceptible to living your life for the sake of others. No company in the world set out without an action plan, a purpose. Your life's purpose is the action plan for your soul. Knowing and working toward your life's purpose brings you a sense of peace and calm that few ever get to experience. When you see your invisible purpose manifesting in the visible world, you feel tangible contentment and joy. Life without purpose feels empty, dull, pointless.

On a societal level, we've overlooked the deep power of purpose. We ought to be teaching the quest for life's purpose in school and in church, beyond instilling education and religion. And yet life's purpose is so specific to each individual that no one can really teach it. You can be taught that it exists, but you have to find it on your own.

Make yourself matter. Do you matter in this world? You must make yourself a priority or you will fade into the status quo and become undetectable except as a walking to-do list lost in the daily grind. Life is far more than just keeping up with it all. We are meant to really live, to express the deepest core of our soul. If you are just getting by, or even getting by very well in the world's eyes but are less than excited about your life, then it is high time you made yourself your number one priority.

The loudest place in the world is a graveyard. There you find talented people who died with their music still hidden inside them, the songs screaming up through the ground. Don't let this happen to you. Your expressions, your talent, your artistic ability and passions, are important to the world. You really matter. You matter to the world. You matter to me, but most importantly you matter to yourself. It is time to start acting like it by making your passions and creative ideas a part of this world. Do more than just survive. Live!

This all sounds fun and exciting, but what often happens is that people too easily scare themselves and revert to the mundane grind of the day-to-day. They do this for fear of not being able to pay the bills if they really follow their dreams. Or too many people are unhappy with their decision and show no support, so the dreamer gives up. This happens when we let the outside world speak more loudly than our inner world. Once we master the power of belief within ourselves, we must tackle the task that too few of us are able or willing to manage, the task of acting on those internal beliefs in the face of opposition and strife. We must quiet the outer senses in such a way as to connect to and live the music of the inner voice.

Unless your inner voice screams at you more loudly than the opposition from the outer voices, which is hardly ever the case at first, then tap into yourself through quiet meditation, prayer, mindfulness, a walk through nature, a shamanic journey or yoga. Calm the outer world so that you can hear what goes on inside you. It is important that as we tap into these quiet spaces we avoid the influence of alcohol or any drugs. Sitting on a calm pond fishing does not do much to connect you to your inner quiet after you've downed a six-pack of beer.

Your very survival depends on you quieting the outside world and hearing your inner purpose and greatness, for "greater is He within you than he who is in the world around you." The one who dwells within needs to be the priority because the outer world will never provide you with support, happiness, peace or serenity. We've all heard the stories of the wealthy husband with the beautiful wife, but he chooses to throw away his marriage on a cheap affair; or there's the massively successful rock star who has it all but kills himself with drugs and alcohol. Though the material realities of countless examples like these are full of wealth and seemingly great things, their inner world imploded. Even those who have everything will want more--more money, more sex, more drugs. What many of us are tricked into believing is that there is a good life out there that will always elude us, so we can never stop trying until we've got enough fame, women or money. If you have lived the surface-only "good life," you know that it did not necessarily provide inner peace of mind. That responsibility is yours and cannot be replaced by material plenty. The inner state of happiness and peace can be yours even if you have not a penny to your name. It is ever within you, and through enough faith and dedication to your inner self, you can know that peace that no one can ever take from you.

Modern societies have placed far too much emphasis on the outer world. It is helpful in some cases to keep a steady eye on the workings of the outer world. We don't feel like rolling out of bed on an early Saturday morning, but our friend calls and wants us to join him on a skiing day trip. Turns out we have a great time by listening to an outer influence poking into our world. External forces sometimes do align with our inner voice and work to our favor, but often they work to our detriment and we resist taking time to examine the difference between positive and negative forces. Notice the positive and negative forces acting on your inner world until it becomes second nature for you to stick to the good while avoiding the bad. Eventually you will naturally live with yourself and your life's purpose as your top priority, keeping the outer world and its influences as a pleasant flavoring to an already fulfilled life.

Life's Purpose as an Expression of Inner Love

We all have innate worth, far more than we often give ourselves credit for. Our society operates on a strict merit system, a mathematical system of plusses and minuses to attach to the good and bad in human behavior. We learn that if we earn enough plusses, if we do enough of the tasks that society deems of value, then we become valuable people. If we get an education, we are more valuable than those who drop out. This fails to paint the whole picture of human worth. We all have innate worth just for being here on this planet together. Nobody asks of the woman who wants to throw herself from the top of a building, "Are you worth being saved? Did you get a good education? Are you an asset to society?" No one asks these questions because at our core we know that it doesn't matter. At our core we know that everyone is valuable and worthy of life. When we act instinctively to save a life, we respond to the core worth in others, a worth that can never be measured by superficial merits.

Another scenario that speaks to the innate worth of others is the love a parent has for her newborn. I remember when I first gave birth to my daughter. I had never felt so much love for a being I had just met. Yet, what had she done to earn my love? What had she done to gain value in the world's merit system? Nothing. In fact, she left my body with stretch marks and even kept me up at nights. Yet the love poured out of me for her. Beneath all the labels and values that the world tries desperately to place on human worth, an unconditional fountainhead of love bubbles up through the surface. We all access this love for each other every time we pursue our life's purpose and influence the lives of others for the better.

By living with the power of unconditional love and against the illusion of merited love, we radiate purpose and self-worth to the world. Some might argue that a person who behaves badly in the world's eyes is bad at their core. You can choose to follow that logic, or you choose to live according to love. Don't busy yourself looking for bad people in the world. Just focus on how you can help people who behave badly to see how they can begin living well. You do this not to enforce the world's merit system but rather to awaken the innate merits that dwell within us all. You make the world a better place not by fixing others but by showing them that they were never broken.

We can move beyond the limitations of "good" and "bad" by tapping into the gap where neither good nor bad exists. In this gap, all things are possible because nothing is impossible. Here we become truly free to be ourselves and to live our lives as soul-directed bodies rather than as body-directed souls. The gap is the place where everything feels alive, creative, fun and free. It may take time to make this shift; and abandoning comfortable labels demands a great deal of trust, but the work is worth it.

You may fear that letting go of good and bad and focusing instead on unconditional love will make you do bad things. Just because you've stopped hating yourself and others for being "bad" does not mean that you accept negative behaviors. You can hate your behavior all day long and still love yourself. Learn to separate your love for yourself and others from the behaviors you observe. No amount of bad behavior will ever make you a bad person, and no amount of good behavior will make you good. It is never your accomplishments that will bring you inner freedom, peace and love. These must be felt from within.

Once you reach the place of non-judgment toward yourself and others, stay in that place by creating your dreams around this new reality. Make it part of your life's purpose to feel unconditional love for yourself and others as you follow the guidance of your dreams.

Wake Up to Yourself

Think for a moment about what it means to have a life's purpose. Really allow this to sink in. It is a huge calling, yet most of us let it pass on by as if it were a pair of shoes or some other nice purchase that could have been. Nothing in your years on Earth will ever matter more than knowing and following your life's purpose. It is your very reason for living, and the way you relate to yourself and others unlocks your power to follow that purpose. You cannot be who you really are in this world unless you radiate your purpose outwards.

A purposeless life demonstrates a lack of connection to ourselves, to others, and to our higher power. Instead, we become as walking to-do lists. We count on external situations to keep our life's ship sailing. We seek temporary comfort, which is really only distraction, in caffeine or by gabbing with friends. All these distractions are screams: "I have no energy! I have no passion of my own, but I don't know where to find it." Sometimes I want to grab these people and shake some of their own life energy back into them, but I cannot. I can only live my life with passion and purpose and radiate my example to others in the hope that they will do the same.

If you lack passion and a life's purpose, then begin at step one. Create for yourself a mission statement. Keep fine tuning the wording that describes your purpose until the words become your very own. Only you will know when your mission has begun. Friends, family and counselors can help you follow it, but no one can ever replace your role as the author of your life. You are irreplaceable in your world. I cannot live your passion for you. It is up to you to find out what it is and to get your life on track by living your purpose once it's found you.

Life's purpose is to our souls as water and sunlight is to plants. Flowers grow full and happy just like we fill ourselves up with purpose. Full of purpose, we no longer feel empty and desperate for drinks, drugs, caffeine, shallow relationships, or any other needling compulsion. Find your purpose before your addiction finds you!

Helping and Being Helped

I've had to return to myself many times in this life. Having slogged through the swamps of pain and hurt, I've discovered that all the years of pain and loss that seemed pointless were forever pointing me in the right direction. By losing myself I learned how to find myself and to keep myself. Through my dark times I have come to share my light with you. This is the essential miracle in my life. All those seemingly wasted years of pain suddenly became healing, educational experiences. All the work I did that seemed like pushing a boulder up a hill only to see it roll down again was in fact a process of growth. It just took longer than my human expectations had hoped on.

After performing an astounding load of inner work I grew accustomed to seeing results manifest in my life very quickly, but there is something about navigating the valleys of grief that draws us far deeper into the darkness than we ever thought possible. The depth of hopelessness and despair was beyond anything I had previously experienced; I certainly knew no way of looking at the loss as empowering. Troy's death dragged me into a grief that outweighed even my fearfully despairing days as a suicidal teen. At least then I felt the touch of God bringing me out of my darkness. After Troy died I felt that even God wasn't listening.

I had to accept that the journey of grief was way bigger than I could ever hope to handle on my own. Every once in a great while we get to see just how vulnerable we are as individuals in this universe. This was such a time for me, a time in which every moment felt purposeless and empty. I had to face up to my limitations and ask for help from others in big ways. The thought of asking for help made my cheeks burn. I had come so far on my own. I used to pride myself on my inner strength and independence. Now all of my old strengths were stripped away. Every hurt I had ever known was exposed again like deep skin beneath a scabby scar. All my trusted defenses were shaken to rubble. To save myself from my life's shipwreck, I had to accept that I was no island.

No person is an island. I know this now. I know it so deeply that I must teach it to you all, especially given the cripplingly individualist society this world has become. If you take every step to enhance your Personal Power (Box One) and eliminate nearly every influence that you have no control over (Boxes Two and Four)--even then you cannot hope to find much fulfillment in life if you see this journey as yours and yours alone. Once you make your light to shine above the darkness, you must share that light with others through the actions of your life's purpose.

Our behaviors impact the lives of others--sometimes for good, sometimes for bad. Our thoughtfulness shows when we take the time to consider how we influence the world. People respond to our consideration by treating us more favorably in return. The opposite is equally true. When we fail to take time to appreciate others, they in turn respond by showing us less consideration.

People are in the world to help each other out. We need only humble ourselves enough to see this. It is often easier to be the helper than the one who needs helped. This is where we become someone else's Box Three, someone else's life's purpose. Your job is to continue asking until you are strong enough to stand in your own power. During my trials of grief, with all my strength and fierce independence blown out the window, I had to keep asking for what I needed until it was no longer necessary. In time I returned to a place where I could stand on my own feet again.

Some people run from the possibility of help, seeking refuge instead in addictions. They sooth themselves with instant gratifications and continue drifting away from the help they need, from themselves. They do not trust that the help they are offered will work for them. They can't abide the thought that they are not in total control as their compulsions drain them of power. Asking for help is the first and often most difficult step when confronting compulsions. In a world that values the elite individual over all else, nobody ever congratulates asking for help. "Oh, you need help. How fantastic!" No, from our earliest years we hear, "Oh, you did it all by yourself. What a big girl!" I'm here to return some value to the power of helping and being helped. It can be empowering to humble ourselves in realizing the value of interconnectedness. Never do we see this more clearly than when we become powerless and need the help of others more than anything. It is humbling to accept the tiny ant-like role we play on this mammoth planet. Even the king of the anthill gets knocked down. We owe it to ourselves to pull ourselves back up.

Every life's purpose relies in some way on helping others. We create meaning in this world by being there when others are lost and powerless. This is because somewhere deep inside we know that we are all one. Healing you, heals me. Countless people have made meaning from significant life losses by helping others through similar tragedies. These acts of healing heal the healers, too. Though this concept conflicts with our individualistic society, helping others deserves at least as much attention as helping ourselves. We certainly need to spend time and energy in Box One, where we bring up our personal power. But once we feel strong in our power, we are responsible for helping others bring up their own personal power levels. Our Box One overlaps with another's Box Three. By helping others, we create more future helpers. It is foolish to only build ourselves up while ignoring the needs of others. Others are in real need, and we can do something positive to heal this world in a big way. We have control over how we treat others. We can start by walking in others' shoes and releasing judgment. We are no islands, but a nation of people helping people. Nobody is here alone.

Making a Choice to Make a Difference

All of us experience dark times as we transition into our lives of purpose. Some days feel hopeless. You've forgotten your purpose and can't remember how to care for yourself or others. I have been through such times, when my behaviors don't quite match who I know I am on the inside. I've done the inner and outer work. I know what I want and make better choices, but the results don't come.

On days when you feel your dream just can't be possible, there might as well be a dark cloud hovering over your life and home. You feel like even the world is against you, and loved ones don't fully support who you are. Let's say you've even fought away the burdens that weigh upon you in Box Two. What now? The answer is to rest while you turn your inner struggles over to your higher power.

Bringing yourself up and out of hopeless despair means releasing unwanted emotions while you follow the path you do want. Holding onto the sufferings in your past is like attempting to hold a beach ball underwater. The negativity will want to pop out through the surface when you least expect it. But if you simply accept and acknowledge the contents of your inner beach ball you can allow them to exit the surface that much more quickly. Notice how much better the child feels after his tantrum's run its course without his parents' fretting over it. Set your tantrums loose, direct your emotional buildup onto inanimate objects like pillows, and then relax. The most important step is the first one you take, so make sure you are walking ahead and not falling back. The path of peace does not have to be silent. You can scream bloody murder and vent the aggression and disappointment of your dark days onto a worthless couch. As long as you clear your dark cloud without hurting yourself or others, you can walk into the light of a new day with less of a burden to bear.

No one expects you to be perfect as you pursue your life's purpose. The path to your best self is not a flat road, a straight line. Its rocky road is rife with curves and blind corners. Good days, great days, bad days, regular days, and down-right horrible days: none of these define who you are as a being. You can link together whatever days come into your life and give that chain deep meaning and power. It matters little how you judge the day; rather, all that matters is what you do with the day. Your dark days gradually clear when you make consistent choices to honor who you really are.

Time will work for or against you depending on the seemingly small choices you make every day. One choice alone appears insignificant, but its effects compound like interest in a savings account. The compounding is more like interest accrued on a revolving credit account, except that in this case the accumulation works in your favor. Your choices carry energetic power to move your world according to your desire. You use this power to your advantage by making choices today according to how you'd like to see your life a year from now.

I like to use the one-year mark as a measure to determine how big or small today's problem really is. If an event today won't factor into my life a year down the road, then I don't sweat it. This is an extension of the "Don't cry over spilt milk" axiom. The same goes for assessing our behaviors. Address what really matters. Don't fret over pointless events today when you could be effecting real growth for yourself. Since we realize that we have so much future ahead of us, we often procrastinate self-improvement. This is the "I'll start tomorrow" syndrome. However, tomorrow will only be worse than today if we fail to address our behaviors and make better choices. We carve grooves into our brains in the form of memories, greasing the rails for negative behaviors to reappear with greater ease in the future. When our choices become so deeply grooved into our brains that they take on a life of their own beyond our ability to choose, we fall into addiction. We do not have to become this far gone, though, if we make proactive choices about our personal growth and inner health.

If we focus on shaping our behaviors according to what we want our lives to look like a year from now, then we input into our brains the material to build the necessary neural pathways. Think of construction workers building a road. The road begins as a rugged path in the thick forest. The more you chip away at the roughage, the easier it is to shape and pave the road. Over time travelers can see the road perfectly and follow its course to their destination with greater ease than had they tried to hack through the forest without the road. Your thoughts circuit down the roads you build in the form of neural pathways in your brain. Don't you want to ensure that the pathways you're building are headed where you want your life to lead? Realize that it is your choices today that create the consequences of your tomorrow.

The smallest right action chips away at a new pathway in your brain, through which new thoughts can flow. You build on this pathway by sending more positive thought energy through. You create your future one thought at a time. You are affecting tomorrow right this second, whether you like it or not. Make sure that you choose thoughts according to how you'd like to end up in the future.

It is crucial to remember that we all are interconnected. The choices you make today empower you to follow your Life's Purpose (Box Three), which leaves a thumbprint on the personal power areas of others (Box One). Thus, you interlock directly with the energies of others in how you choose to effect the world. In the same way, your Box Two events overlap with the Box Four of others, providing them with distractions that do neither of you any good to spend too much time and energy on. Our Grids connect with others in this way, in an endless chessboard of overlapping energetic Boxes. Find and follow how your can best influence the lives around you. The more you can extend love into the network of overlapping grids, the better your chances of changing the whole world. The love you extend becomes the love another extends to another, and to another, and so on.

You are not alone. Somewhere out there is someone who feels or who has felt just as you feel. When we begin to really hear and see each other's hearts, we become understood. When we are understood, we can let go of our attachment to the dark clouds that float through our days. By needing each other and by being needed, we begin to make a positive difference in the life of the world. Start today.

Chapter 6

Eliminating Distractions

Cut the Chatter

You know what you want, but you hesitate. You've found your purpose and know what you want to do with your life. So what's stopping you? You're stopping yourself, but you think others are doing it to you. You allow the senseless chatter and judgments of others to derail you from yourself. But their negativity is never powerful enough to pull you off course. It is you who derail your own dream when you give more power to the pettiness of others than it deserves.

Let's say you want to be a singer. You know there are people in the world who also want this, who want to be rock stars. You see them as more talented, and perhaps you meet people who criticize you for wanting to make a star of yourself. They think you don't have what it takes. This ought to be nothing to you, but you accept their words and deny yourself. Cut this out. The opinions of others fall squarely into Box Four of the Energetic Management Grid. They have no power over you whatsoever. You cannot control the skill level of others, or whether they think you have what it takes or not. You can only control your own progress toward your dream. And yet, too many of us allow the petty energies of Distractions to destroy our dreams because we falsely believe we can never be as good as others. We use the successes of others to justify making premature failures of ourselves. We drain our power from Box One into Box Four, which deserves none of our greatness. We surrender our power before we ever get a chance to feel it. We give up our own dreams before we get a chance to live them.

No matter how talented and rich the people are in your Box Four, you will never feel such richness unless you manifest it from within. Living vicariously through others' successes, including those of friends and close loved ones, can last only so long. Eventually comes the day when you must answer for what you have done for you.

Can you say that you lived your life with the intention of living your truth while eliminating all outside distractions? Looking to what's wrong or right about the outside world is a way of denying your own inner truth. Pushing against the world's flaws drains you of valuable energy that you ought to apply to areas that you actually can control. People shouldn't steal, for example. This is a fact that all people agree on; yet the reality is that theft is happening right now. Our attitude of "This shouldn't be!" as we push against the world's imperfections drains our power and we move away from our inner work. We can't do everything about all the suffering in the world, and if we fall beneath the sufferings in Box Four we guarantee that we will never be able to help the world.

Distractions can sometimes bridge us to action. We read the social climate from there. We check in with the news of the world so we can know what's going on at present, but we ought not to dwell there for good. Give only about 10 percent of your energy to matters that you don't control and which don't influence you. It's good to know about the pains and joys in the world, but get back to your own inner work once you know. Otherwise you become a victim to the world and its ways.

Most of us will at times actually create noise as a way to ignore what's really going on inside of us. Our noisemaking catches up to us eventually. As my supervisor in graduate school always says, you can turn around and face it or let it trip you from behind. We peg pain and trauma as being intrinsically bad for us, so we mask what's real by falling into distracted patterns. Pain--whether it is emotional, physical, psychological, or spiritual--signals us to slow down and change our behaviors. You wouldn't look at a stop sign as a bad thing. Signposts save lives, and the same goes for the pain signals inside you. You can either read and heed the signs' warnings or risk accidents as you drive on with the car radio on full blast. The world offers enough distractions without you having to add to them.

If there is simply more than you can cope with going on inside of you, seek outside support. Otherwise you risk living a life forever at the whim of inner and outer noise. You may feel yourself the helpless victim of needling distractions. For example, you may wonder why others can have a drink or two in a night and not succumb to alcoholism like you have. Or, why can some people splurge on pizza and ice cream one night and then go back to healthy eating the next day while this feels impossible to you? If you lose control where others manage to remain steady, you need to strengthen your responses to your energetic signposts. You can greatly reduce your life's distracting chatter by not contributing to it from within.

We look for external reasons to explain why we've grown so distracted; we point fingers at visible enemies, but the real enemy is the neglected friend inside of us who is attempting furiously to lead us back to our true selves. At this stage, nearly none of the distractions we face in the form of negativity and criticism are really outside of us. If they were, then we would all be puppets to the outside noise. It would be common and expected to scream and strike at others when they oppose us, but of course not everybody does this. Quit contributing to Distractions in Box Four by making a choice. You have the power to choose or to avoid anger, hatred and resentment. Bring your unconscious negative responses to the conscious surface of your being. This can be as seemingly impossible as attending to a whisper inside a blaring rock concert. Your life's noise may be cranked up so loud that you cannot tell where you contribute to the noise and where the actual noise of the world begins. Though this demands that you pay close attention to what's going on both in and around you, the rewards more than justify the effort.

If you fail to distinguish between inner and outer noise, you miss out on more than the messages of your soul. You set your life on a collision course, and few people if any will show surprise when you crash. You will lose control when you live without heeding your inner messages. You are much more than just one of the many ants making the world work by taking your humble place on the anthill. You're an individual, a powerful human being with thoughts and feelings. If your inner voice does not matter to you, then they won't be taken seriously by anyone else in this world.

You matter. You have value and greatness beyond your own comprehension. Give yourself a chance to really exist in this world without the constraints of inner or outer noise. Really pay attention to yourself. If nothing else, fake it until you make it!

Of the many thoughts that pass through your mind in an average day, a great proportion of them are not your own. They came in through the media, adults, authority figures, and your community. Memes, behaviors that replicate through observation and imitation, behave like mind viruses, "infecting" individuals to copy the behaviors and attitudes that swarm around their heads. In school, children replicate the thoughts and attitudes of peers and teachers. Belief teaching is another form of meme replication. Religions commonly teach others what to believe and, quite often, how to believe it. Certain societal "truths" become commonly accepted as social dogmas. There is a meme that has stubbornly carried through the decades that insists women must fall downhill after age 40 in terms of looks. Some even accept that women are all used up after 30. Is this really true? Or is it only accepted? When we hear a thing enough times, no matter how silly it may be, we come to accept it as truth. If enough people from a society accept a thought as a belief and replicate that belief on a large enough scale, then it becomes "truth." This, however, only makes the thing true in theory, not in fact. It's only an accepted truth that women are downhill after 40, but in fact women can be vivacious however the hell long they want to be. The problem is that so many people push commonly accepted truths to further their own agenda. If a makeup company can ride the wave of thought that hammers into the common mind that aging is a disgrace and something to be avoided at all costs, then consumers will spend billions of dollars on their anti-aging products. Thus memes, the chatter of external beliefs that have infiltrated the individual's mind, contribute to the profits of a few at the expense of most.

This is why outer noise must be cranked down. We may never know the precise origin of every thought that floats through us, but we can never know what our own thoughts ought to be until we spend ample time in mental quiet. Until we do this we will also be unable to contribute to communities and to the world around us. As long as we continue falling prey to the noise of external beliefs, which is often the noisiest energy of all, the rest of the world will always be perfectly capable of crushing us beneath its chatter. We must block this out as best we can. Thankfully we do control how we block the noise, even if we cannot control the content of the noise itself. We can switch off the TV from infiltrating our homes with its belief barrage. We can put down the magazine or let the phone sit idle for an evening or two. We can spend this quiet time instead focusing on purifying our own inner noise. By doing this we embrace the wisdom of our own silence and discover the true identity of our thoughts, beliefs, intuition, and inner genius.

Think Your Own Thoughts

Everyone has an inner genius, one that knows what it wants and how to get it. When we eliminate distractions and begin living as ourselves and not through others, our genius awakens to drive our lives. The genius is built from the unique life experiences of each individual, so no two are exactly alike. Think about that for a moment. No person on Earth carries the same life history as you do. Some may bear striking similarities to you, but nobody can know what it means for you to be you. Therefore it is you and you alone who can know how to bring about your life's fulfillment. That said, adopting generic belief systems poses a great danger because they cannot fit you perfectly. People will try selling you on certain beliefs, such as accepting the false truth that you need a particular makeup to feel sexy. Cosmetic companies are experts on cosmetics; only you are the expert on you. Unless and until you open to your inner genius by eliminating distractions in your world, you permit the media and other corporations to direct your life.

Energy is Irreplaceable

Where did the time go? When we invest our energies into others' business and gossip, we lose a precious commodity that we could have spent enriching our own lives. Before you line up to waste your energies attending to the latest Distractions in Box Four (i.e., news stories of spoiled celebrities, the way others talk about you), ask yourself if you would spend money in this way. For example, would you throw money into the latest scoop on Brad Pitt and Angelina Jolie? Or would you pay others to gossip about you in ways that can't build you up? The people and influences in Box Four will always be around; they don't need your money, so they certainly don't need your irreplaceably valuable energy.

You need your energy far more than others need it. Why waste it on those who do nothing with it? Don't cast these precious pearls to the wind, no matter how enticing the distractions may seem. Chances are your distracted state is nothing more than a wakeup call to pull yourself back into your own dreams and power.

The only positive effect that gossip seems to have is its ability to minimize the fallibility of those who follow the gossip. This is precisely why we keep up with the latest celebrity dirt and the hot scoop around the office water cooler. It provides a mask, a false means for feeling better about our own situation. The problem is that this sense of feeling better is fleeting at best. We quickly return to emptiness whenever we remember that Box Four Distractions do nothing to empower our lives in any meaningful way. And as our time wastes away before our eyes, our emptiness couples with a desperate feeling that we'll never amount to anything. The longer we empty ourselves to distractions, the more biting will be this feeling of helplessness.

By cutting away the distractions that suck our energies, we rediscover lost time. Time is the plane on which our energies take shape. Steal your life away from the energy suckers by demanding more from life. Quit investing in habits and friendships that only take from you. Instead of investing in others who will never invest in you, put this energy back toward yourself and your greater purpose.

A lack of time is always the primary excuse we use to justify not exercising our dream muscle. We think we can't find the time, but we'd be shocked to discover just how much of our precious time is lost in a wasteland. Our lives feel aimless and pointless whenever we give our time and attention to nothingness, to meaninglessness. People who live their dreams do not waste a single moment, and thus they never feel aimlessness and hopelessness creeping in.

The goal here is not to be perfect, but rather to improve by following the example of those who live their dreams. I still get caught up by the trap of attractive time wasting. But awareness equals improvement!

Guilt, shame, and self-loathing are also quick and easy ways to avoid embracing and expressing our greatness. Fight for yourself. Fight until the greatness that wants to get out, gets out and becomes who you are in every aspect. Be great in body, in mind, in spirit, and with others. You are well worth the fight against the crippling Distractions of Box Four. I believe in your ability to rise above and be you. I love you.

Chapter 7

My Personal Energy Management Practice: Unleashing My Inner Sex Goddess

One practical application of the Energy Management Grid for me is found in my feminine psyche. What used to fill me with shame and suck me into dangerous approval cycles was my sexual identity and sexual self-expression. I had to learn to make friends with the woman (goddess) within in order to accept my shadow self and all of the socially acceptable parts of me. Through a long process of getting to know myself as a sensual being, as well as letting go of unobtainable ideals of womanhood, I began to gain energy by connecting to the sensual woman inside of me. For fun, I call her my Inner Sex Goddess. She can be found in us all, of that I am certain.

The Sex Goddess is an Energy

All women, independent of others, share the inalienable right to express their innate sexuality. Any and every woman has the power inside of her to feel beautiful, sexy and free. Sexiness is an energy, a feeling that comes from within. There it depends not upon anyone but the woman it belongs to. The woman's responsibility is to connect with the feeling within and then vibrate that outward on the level of sexual energy.

Every woman in the world has the capacity to feel like a Marilyn Monroe without setting foot outside her home. Outside approval is irrelevant and only distracts the woman from who she is inside. We women are sexual beings and ought to feel sexy whenever we feel like it. Sexual energy rejuvenates us, inspires us and causes us to feel a greater intensity for life that we cannot know without accessing the passion within.

The challenge arises when we fail to allow ourselves to feel sexy just for us. Society today says that the guy must determine what is sexy. The press defines sexuality as an external phenomenon to be felt by only a scant few women who are fortunate enough to grace a magazine cover. It is time to take sexy away from being something beyond us and return it to its rightful dwelling place, within us. We all have equal access to sexual power and energy, just as we all have the ability to experience joy in our lives on a daily basis.

Get yourself to feel so hot and sexy that you want to have sex with yourself. I'm not talking about masturbation here. This is falling in love with yourself in a whole new and deeper way. Just as the lessons in self-love awaken your soul power, the lessons in unleashing the sex goddess from within will awaken your enlivening sexual power.

Just as there are certain behaviors that bring joy into our lives, certain behaviors awaken our sexual power. First and foremost, this must come from within. Despite the way the world looks at sexuality, you must awaken this power for no one else but yourself. This does not mean that your partner will not benefit from the awakening. It simply means that your partner's enjoyment of this power is secondary to its awakening in you.

When you feel sexy just for yourself, you fill up your own cup. You give the most powerful energy in the world back to yourself instead of pouring it out to others like too many woman tend to do. Don't give the power away as soon as you feel it. This is being sexy for someone else's benefit, or only for a particular occasion. Others can soak in your abundance once you've built up enough within yourself that you can offer it outwards. There is enough sexual energy to go around.

You can connect to this powerful energy on a daily basis. Let it fill and reenergize you. Too many women are doing way too much. They busy themselves with work, home, and kids. They lose track of the great energy force within them because it does not seem an urgent pressing need. There is a reason why the earliest carved representations were artworks of the feminine form. The female sexual power is so captivating, so enlivening, it moves whole civilizations to radiate their inner art. Make the expression of your sexual goddess an urgent need and notice how the rest of your life falls into balance.

When I was with Troy I would wear some sexy clothes and dance to candlelight with the music of my choice. Although he was there as a passive observer, he allowed me the space and freedom to dance for myself and to allow my own sexuality to flow into the room. It did not matter that I weighed 180 pounds and had just given birth, or that my breasts were sagging and my stomach was traced with stretch marks. The point was not to look good or to be sexually impressive from the guy's perspective. The point was to be free and to let go of the world, to connect with a power larger than myself. I felt beautiful inside. I felt free.

I wanted to feel this way again and again until I began connecting with it at many times and in many places. I would feel the power radiating through me when while I picked out new clothes or while envisioning myself in the future. I became skinnier, sexier and freer on a regular basis. We do not and cannot beat ourselves into feeling good. It simply does not work this way. Feeling tired and exhausted will only leave you feeling more tired and exhausted until you change your way of life. Even after a tough day of work, sure I would not lift another finger, I found my secret hiding place against the world right inside my own home. My home became more than the four walls that surrounded me at night. I felt at home within my own body. All the problems of the world disappeared as I began dancing. I'd close my eyes and move, and the day's complaints grew increasingly irrelevant. The world's demands could not touch me inside my body's cradling home.

I soon realized that this safe place of powerful sexual energy could not be exclusive to me. All women must have access to this magical land within, but why didn't they access it and express it? If they could only know the regenerating benefits of the inner sex goddess, surely they would take the time to unleash her. Also, I bet people would stop looking outside themselves to the Internet, drugs or alcohol for fulfillment if they felt their own capacity to enrich and excite their own lives.

As with most things that are good for you, change comes gradually. When I first stepped into the new "me" role, I remember feeling awkward, embarrassed and angry with myself for not being perfect or for letting myself go for as long as I had. I can beat myself up with the best of them. However, thankfully I realized that beating myself up would lead me nowhere. I pressed on through the discomfort, and I'm so grateful I did. It was then that I found this wealth of untapped energy right inside of me, just waiting to be uncovered and set free. You have this energy within you as well. It waits for you to stop judging against yourself, to stop cutting yourself short because of trepidation and embarrassment.

There is nothing embarrassing about living as a sexual being. You can use positive judgment to figure out what is safe as you begin tapping into your sexual power. But once you know you are safe, be sure to put judgment away so that you can release your inner sex goddess. The goddess cannot coexist with self-doubt and criticism. Further, even if you judge yourself and like what you see, there is no place even for this. Energy is neither good nor bad. It simply is. You simply are. You throw yourself off balance when you see yourself as sexy with any eyes other than your own. External good looks aren't fulfilling. They are the product of luck and good genes. Unleashing the sex goddess is about transcending the physical flesh to tap into something far more profound. It is not about seeing yourself as hot; it is about feeling the heat within your own soul!

The First Lesson -- Know Yourself

Discover something that heightens your sexuality. It must resonate within you. Don't ignore small signals. The guidance you seek will come only as whispers at first. Stretch yourself out of your comfort zone. Try on clothes you would never normally try on. You seek a tiny burst of excitement, an energy increase within you that feels good in response to the experience it desires. Allow the energy to flow through you and guide you to what it wants. Your job is to sit back and listen.

You may have been disconnected from this part of yourself for some time, or you may have overruled it by following what you supposed other people want from you. When you take others' supposed wants before your own, you allow others to trample your energy. If the people around you truly care about who you are as a being, they will ultimately want you to be happy. Too often we cut ourselves off from our own gifts because of the ideas we have about what others expect from us. When we live in the here and now and know our own gifts deeply, the only expectation we will feel is to radiate our power to the world.

Being a sex goddess is about feeling good from the inside out. People can see inside of us whether or not we think they can. We may fool them for a while, but we all expose ourselves eventually. Before doing anything else in this world, we need to take the time to truly love ourselves at our core. This means getting to know ourselves, being good to ourselves and being gentle with ourselves. In fact, loving yourself evolves in much the same way as falling in love with a significant other.

First, you spend time getting to know yourself. You may choose to step into nature as a means of tapping into your core, the deepest part of yourself that tries to hide beneath your exterior. Find the core of your being that only wants to be loved. Show yourself love by thinking positive thoughts into yourself. Focus on everything you like about yourself. Practice acceptance and non-judgment. Treat yourself as you would want others to treat you. Finally, forgive yourself as you would forgive others. Your beauty will never shine from your core and out through your surface self if you harbor even the slightest self-resentment. Give yourself a hug, tell yourself you are okay, and radiate that joy to others.

Meaningful self-time is much more than simply being alone. Alone, we can still distract ourselves with TV, the Internet and the phone. There are millions of ways to be alone but not really alone. You won't get to know yourself if you remain stuck with distractions. It is inside those truly alone and intensely quiet moments that we come to know ourselves on a deep level. You can achieve this state through prayer, meditation, mindfulness, going on an "information vacation," keeping a journal, or taking a nature retreat.

You will never love yourself until you know yourself!

The Second Lesson -- Become Your Own Best Friend

Rededicate yourself daily to self-love. Your relationship with yourself is nearly as critical as your relationship with your higher power. How you treat yourself is vitally more important than even how you treat others, including loved ones. There is a good reason why even mothers need to affix their own lifesaving mask during a plane crash before helping their children: without first saving themselves, they cannot hope to save their children. Without loving yourself, you cannot share much or any love with others.

I propose that the deeper you love yourself, the deeper and more authentically you will love others, including your children and loved ones. Loving yourself requires treating yourself with kindness, affection and encouragement. Become your own best friend. Are you friendly with yourself right now? Do you speak to yourself in the way a friend would speak to you? If not, call yourself out on it. Say to yourself that derogatory self-talk will not be tolerated. If you haven't known any positive role models of good friendship, you can create one by setting your own standard of friendship. Care about yourself enough to give yourself what you need and deserve. Stop ignoring your own wants and desires in order to please others. Martyrdom is best left for sainthood; so unless you're planning to become a saint, leave self-sacrifice out of the equation.

The world wants more than just a part of you. The world wants everything you have to offer, but you can't give it if you deny yourself in the false hope of making other people happy. Let go of the false ideals you've clung to about being a "better" person. Get real and accept yourself as you are. Don't be afraid to acknowledge your dreams, desires, likes and dislikes. Allow the inside of you to communicate with the world outside. This may feel painful at first, especially if you find yourself in pain on the inside. Don't let the pain scare you into self-hiding. Don't fear what you find; walk straight into it. Learn from what your insides want to teach you about yourself.

What story does your pain have to tell? What lessons can you learn from deep self-exploration? When people slow down long enough to feel the intensity of their pain, they often do everything they can to avoid feeling the pain again. Avoidance of real pain is a grave mistake and a way to dissociate from reality. Reality is real; you cannot succeed in running from it because it will always catch up with you. The only gray area here is how big it will be when it gets you. Don't let inner pains and problems grow out of control. No amount of pretending is going to make it go away. What does dissipate the pain is stopping and allowing the pain to surface before cleaning it up.

Stop running from yourself. The first step you take is a time-out. Call "pause" on your life. People do this all the time in counseling sessions: one-hour time-out breaks. The drawback here is that it often can be too little, too late by the time we start asking for help. Don't permit things to fester inside until they are bigger than you can handle. Get help now! Do not wait another day. When you think your life cannot get any worse, sometimes it can. There is no sense in waiting for total breakdown and desperation. If your insides need attention, it is you who ultimately need to give that attention. Be your own best friend and you will free the inner goddess from the shackles of personal despair.

The Third Lesson -- Judge Not, Lest Your Soul Pay the Price

Judgment is a useful quality when applied correctly. When used incorrectly, it is a powerful soul killer that destroys the artistic seeds of the dreamer before they ever get the chance to grow. I often wonder how much of our art and music stays stuck inside us because of this one terrifying ability we have, called judgment.

Judgment employed in the right away and in the right circumstance keeps us safe and steers us from poor choices. Good judgment can save lives and increase the quality of life. It can help a business to grow wealth and keeps a marriage united. However, as is the belief of many Americans, if a little is good, then more must be even better! Such is far from the case with judgment. We've somehow let judgment run rampant in our society today because of the good it can offer. When we do this, our souls pay the price. Self-expression is the soul's food, and judgments that manifest as crippling criticisms only ever starve the soul.

In art, music, writing and dancing, when we allow judgment (usually thrown at us by others) to override our soul's expression, we shut off the light source within us. Maslow's peak experiences, those uplifting transcendent events that direct and define a lifetime, depend on the soul's sustenance. Negative judgment creates a famine that gets far too little press today.

Our souls need time and freedom from judgment's famine just as our bodies rely on food and water. If you've become bored with the mundane phenomena in this world, chances are that you've allowed your mind, the organ of judgment, to silence your inner music. Your mind will try to trick you by saying you don't have what it takes, that soul expression is best left to "professionals." This is when the critical energy hog of the mind, the ego, dominates and locks the soul deeper in the dungeon.

Ego loves comparisons. The fastest way to tell if you are coming from ego is to notice yourself making comparisons. Are you comparing yourself to others and considering yourself better or worse? Whether you see yourself as better or worse, your soul has become a victim of the ego's need to compare and criticize. If others are better, then you beat yourself up for being not enough. If others are worse, you contrive a false sense of superiority that rests on the one condition that you remain better than them. Neither of these scenarios feed the soul. Indeed, they feed the ego at the soul's expense. If you are worse than everyone else, then there is no need for the soul to even try expressing itself. If you are better than everyone else, you never really feel the soul's expression because the ego is so busy screaming in your ear to remain above the rabble. Such "success" rides on conditions.

Judgment depends on others for its existence. Love of the soul depends only on you and your willingness to sing your inner music no matter what the ego or the outside world wants. All you need do in this life is to express the song of your soul. Peak experiences aren't met by accident. When you establish your soul as the center of your life, you'll find all your days brimming with peak experiences. There are people out there truly living their dream lives, ecstatically happy and energized by following their life's great purpose. They've not abandoned judgment entirely. No, they see its uses and judge how to order their material world so that the life of their soul can remain their primary expression.

I learned to live a life full of soul expression when Troy first taught me how. It's all about feeling a sense of inner freedom. We must follow what feels good and right to us from a centered place. We then follow where the feeling leads. It can be just that simple. Olympic athletes begin with nothing more than a passion for their sport, which they practice over and over again until an inner shift occurs. Their outer life and their inner passion become one. We don't need to be champions in the world's eyes or take home gold medals, but we all must eliminate judgment and follow our passions if we hope to awaken the flowing beauty within.

The Power of the Goddess

The goddess's power enables you to assert physical control over your life. The goddess awakens the dream within, yet too many of us think dreams are far too childish and fleeting. Your dream is more than a child's wish that flees when you become an adult. The world is your playground, and there is no sense in raking up the leaves while growing resentful at all the people having fun on the swings or the monkey bars. Young, old, and in between: freedom and fun are for all of us. Sexiness is within each and every one of us. We've fallen so far out of touch from our innately sensual natures; the more we try to suppress our sexual power, the more it pops up as addictions or personal catastrophes.

I say it is high time to take back control and let the goddess express her power as we align with our true natures. We are sexual beings. It is more than okay to feel sexy, to experience the sensuality that comes from within. If you try to act like it doesn't exist, you sap a life-given energy granted to us by God. Suppressing such innately healthy urges does not help you to gain energy. Instead, you lose energy by forcing yourself to be a passionless being, which you are not.

You may have legitimate reasons to want to suppress your innate sexuality. Perhaps you have been hurt by sexual acts in the past. If this is true, then I encourage you to take great strides to resolve these issues so that you too can connect to and release this wellspring of physical and spiritual power.

As a society, we've become so afraid of being sexually immoral that we routinely downplay our sexual identity. How has this worked for us? We are at an all-time immoral high with sexual depictions circulating through the media. Sexual affairs as well as intellectual and emotional affairs have become common because we've externalized sex instead of feeling it from within us. Sex is something you see in the store or on TV or access through the Internet. But we never needed any of these sources or even other people to tap into our own sexual power that is far from immoral. I'm talking about connecting to the sexual being within, sensing her power, and allowing her the space to exist as part of you in this world. We carry far too many roles in this life: parent, worker, friend, spouse. We busy ourselves with outer labels while we miss our own bodily power.

You can be the star of your own private blockbuster hit. Make your days count by taking care of the celebrity you are. Respond to her wants, her deepest desires, passions and needs. Too often as women, we respond to everyone else's needs first before taking our own into account. We make stars out of our children or our spouses. If we were meant to take others first, we would have been born inside their bodies. Instead, we try to approximate the experience of living through others. We don't live inside their bodies, but we ignore our own. We lose touch with our power to advocate on our behalf, to express the beauty that hides within us. I urge you right now to take that power back. It's not too late.

Breaking Through the Noise

So, if your sex goddess is not on your side, where is she hiding? She is still within you. She's just been clouded by society and the outer Distractions of Box Four. Sound unfair? It is! She is talking away, but you have surrendered to the noise for so long that she might as well not have a voice at all.

Give her back her voice. This is where genuine self-empowerment comes from. Create a new definition of sexiness for yourself, one that doesn't rely on the external world. Make the definition accessible and intuitive for you, since you are the only one it matters to. There dwells in all women a sex goddess, an energy that provides us with unbelievable potential, excitement, and enthusiasm. You need only listen to her through the mad shouting of the crowd. So many of us do not even see ourselves anymore. We go about the world like walking to-do lists, neither enjoying life nor really living it. We can satisfy our to-do lists, but at what cost? The time to start living, loving, and enjoying life is right now!

I frequently unleash the goddess in my own life by dressing up in scant clothing, wearing high heels, and dancing. I've also found it helpful to be in the present moment as I admire my legs, breasts, and face. Taking time to admire this body that I was given encourages and energizes me to take more care of myself. This creates a self-perpetuating cycle of self-care and admiration that depends on nothing outside of me to keep going.

Admiration is crucial. What good can you do yourself if you're a beautiful woman but cannot enjoy that for yourself? On the flipside, you can be a woman the world considers unattractive, but you are truly beautiful if you admire yourself every day. The more I admire myself, the more others magically begin to make notice of the care I give to myself.

It may seem conceited at first to admire yourself, but this is not the goal here. You do this with the intention of noticing and caring for the beauty in you. This goes deeper than the beauty on your surface. You admire yourself to your deepest core. What a treat it can be for a lady to be adored. I propose that we are independent of anything or anyone outside of us; we can adore ourselves.

All humans crave validation. We need to know that we are heard and really understood. We also derive validation from being seen. Otherwise, wouldn't we solely listen to musical performances? Why watch the orchestra as it plays? Wouldn't we only talk to friends over the phone? Why do we hang children's drawings on the fridge? Being seen--displaying ourselves and our art--is a powerful means of validation.

If you are unaccustomed to being seen, then the concept of validation may be foreign to you. Don't think for a second that you need others to validate you. Feel validated, feel empowered, by radiating attention to yourself. Do you appreciate yourself? Do you see yourself? Spend time looking at yourself in the mirror. Wear clothes that you like. Move in ways that excite you. You matter. Reflect love onto yourself until you habitually get excited about the person you see in the mirror. Take time to soak yourself in. Allow yourself to feel this excitement welling up until you generate more than enough to power the beauty of your body. This is real sexual energy. You can access it at any time because it comes from you and you alone. Enjoy it. Spend time every day accessing it until it becomes second nature. When you are comfortable in your own skin, you can share this energy with the one you love if you so choose. If your partner does not see or validate you at first, give it time. Remember that you may not see yourself without great practice. It takes time and effort to see the beauty within, especially in the world that thrives on fleeting surface attractions. Let go of the external struggle to gain the eyes of the world by realizing that all the visual validation you need comes from within.

How I Lost Her--How I Found Her Again

After Troy's death, I felt like the spirited, happy, sexy lady I had been, was now dead. I wanted to find her again, to slice through the layers of both physical and emotional weight. She was on the other side of my grieving self, behind the darkness somewhere. She had been such fun, and I still loved her. I had loved watching her shine through me. Sometimes she really impressed me in surprising ways. I missed feeling good about myself, missed wearing bright colors instead of depressing black and brown. I missed feeling light, free, bubbly, and full of energy and life.

Would I ever see her again? Would I ever feel her in my days? The thought of never again being able to feel so free was as damning as a life prison sentence, except this prison was my own lethargic, bored, and empty body. I couldn't bear being so unhappy, knowing that she was still there locked up deep inside. I couldn't stand watching others living their dreams without singing the song of my own soul. I still believed in dreams, but I needed more than the words to pull me through. I didn't want to stop at believing. I used to experience it; it had been so real to me. Somehow I slipped away from myself as life energies became more thoroughly absorbed inside Boxes Two (his death devastated me, and I was powerless to prevent the event) and Four (people will ridicule me if I express my dreams to them).

As long as my focus remained planted in the powerless Boxes, I was sure to avoid what was staring me right in the face, desperate to express itself: my very own power to create and to dream. My cheeks burn when I think about my self-avoidance. How could I have been so close to that power and yet millions of miles away from it in my power to act? The time had come to quit avoiding personal responsibility to manifest my power. Oh yes, I was ready to live again. Nobody ever told me, however, how hard it would be to regain that life. It would mean giving up all the addictions I had come to lean on. I had to give up mochas and junk food, say no to parties, change my diet, leave my job, and draw boundaries at home.

With tears in my eyes, I began a new struggle. It was incredibly difficult to take responsibility for her now. I had let my goddess decline for so long. I had inflicted too much damage and created too many bad habits. Habitual fear and hopelessness made me doubt that I could get her back. I needed help, but I knew inside that ultimately, like Norman Vincent Peale says: "If it is to be it is up to me." It was my own mess, and it was my responsibility to clean myself up. Where to start?

Addictions. Addictions reinforce our feelings of powerlessness, tricking us to false feelings of comfort only to leave us clawing for them through the dark future. My addiction to coffee also contributed significantly to my weight gain. It was necessary for me to start there in retrieving my lost power. The coffee addiction began the very day after Troy's death. I started drinking eight cups of tea a day and immediately switched over to coffee because tea was not quite strong enough. I had no energy coming from within, so I sought this very available vice to get myself moving. Then came the sugar, added to the coffee. Oh, how I seemed to feel better when I felt the combined sugar-caffeine buzz. I could pull myself out of bed. I could do the dishes. I could drive my daughter to school. Instead of asking for real help, I decided to seek this false help on my own. When the sugar-caffeine buzz was unavailable, there were painkillers around to numb my daily devastation. The real nightmare descended when I realized permanently that he was gone, no matter how vain I struggled to cease the pain. Sugar and caffeine were my noble saviors, or so I thought. The damage crept in with silent subtlety at first. I tried crying out for help, but no one will ever get worried when you tell them you're hooked on coffee and sugar. Join the line! These addictions are too commonplace for anyone to stage interventions over, so I continued chipping away the beautiful woman I had been. The erosion happened slowly, but in time I bought into the false belief that I could heal but never get back to that sexy energetic being I had been.

That is until I had a friend remind me that I'm worth fighting for; the vivacious me within, who overpowers her addictions, is worth fighting for! I'm worth getting my life back. I made the extreme decision thanks to his help, support, and encouragement, to quit the counseling job I enjoyed and focus my lost energies on me. My Personal Power of Box One had been empty for far too long. I had no idea what it meant to be my primary focus. All I had was a memory, a fleeting memory of a lost person. I didn't know how at first, but I knew I was going to try to find her and free her from the chains that had bound her.

This return certainly didn't happen overnight. I was chronically exhausted from taking care of everyone else in my world except me. At first I just needed rest. I felt guilty about getting rest because I could only think about the needs of everyone else. My needs--the needs that mattered more than all else--were difficult for me to meet without these significant twinges of guilt.

Then I felt lost. I busied myself with things that didn't interest me because it provided false relief from the hard road ahead of me: a steep climb that meant losing 60 pounds and living out my dream of writing a book to reach your heart and soul. I didn't believe in myself at first. After all, it was me who got me into this mess in the first place. How could I ever trust myself after that? Self-disbelief is a sure way to kill action. I think most great achievements in this life require 90 percent belief and 10 percent action. The greater the action, the greater the required self-belief. I had big dreams. I was going to need that much more belief, but I felt I had none left.

How could I gain something I had lost so completely? How could I learn to believe in myself when I always had Troy to believe in me? The equation demands faith. You start by choosing to create self-belief and then move toward that in the arms of your higher power. Thus, CHOICE + FAITH = REAL BELIEF. It takes a certain bit of divine intervention, but you first have to choose that you want it. Others couldn't hand their self-belief over to me; I had to ask for it. I had to ask a power beyond myself to radiate through me until I learned to believe in myself enough to do it on my own.

You have to ask for what you lack. Life doesn't operate through magic or accident. Asking is how you make the seemingly random become quite deliberate. Once you ask from a depth of faith in a positive result, the fruits of your seeking will become reality.

Asking for what I wanted helped bring me into a haven of self-belief and dream expression. There still remained the task of protecting myself and my dreams from critical non-believers. Shockingly, most of this unbelief stems from within because others can do precious little to derail your dreams. The critics within do enough damage to replace a whole globe full of sneers. This is where boundaries become crucial--boundaries against the world outside, boundaries against the world within.

Protecting my sex goddess from interior criticism is necessary to her growth and expression. You might even say self-protection is as important as self-nurturance. Nurture and protect. We do the same with children and pets. It's not complicated. Life can make it complicated by throwing endless methods at us. Just as there are countless ways to raise a child and raise her well, there are countless ways to nurture and protect your inner power. This is where you step out as your expert on you. Only you will know the answer when you hear it.

When training to be a counselor, I was relieved to discover that I didn't have to know all the answers. Further, the idea of a right answer varies greatly from person to person. I can encourage you to take up the journey of personal growth and expression, but it is entirely up to you to do the work. Never doubt your self-expertise. You are the whole judge and jury. You get to decide what works for you and in what direction you wish to point your life. This can be easy to forget in a society that feeds on dodging responsibility. The buck stops with you!

Feel-Good Your Way There

How did I lose the weight and reawaken my sex goddess in ways I could not have imagined? I did not do it by feeling bad or by punishing myself. No. I "feel-gooded" my way there. I quit hiding who I was inside. Reach for feeling good. Stand in the line that leads to feeling good. You cannot "feel-bad" your way to healing. It is possible to feel bad long enough that you hit rock bottom and then decide to do whatever it takes to get better. However, you do not have to do this. You can decide today to feel-good your way there instead. You can decide to change your life for the best, to reach for something better right this very second!

Energies attract similar energies. Dress your best every single day. When you dress better, you attract better feelings from inside you. We are all familiar with downward spirals. Why not do good to yourself and follow an upward spiral? Once you have completed the inner healing work, it is high time for the upward spiral to take effect. When people would ask how I lost weight the second time around, I responded with, "I feel-gooded my way into it." I bought clothes I felt good in, even though I swore I wouldn't waste my money. I fixed up my hair and put on nice makeup and jewelry, even though I was going nowhere special that day. You have to train your body into a whole new way of feeling and being. You have to let your body know what it wants to feel so it will know what to look for. If you've never felt good about your physical self, then get a makeover of your choosing.

Every woman is beautiful. We all have admirable qualities. It is just a matter of taking notice and highlighting what we see. Instead of hiding what you don't want, accentuate what you do want. If you focus on all that you find negative about yourself and your body, you are not going to care much about self-care. Quit doing this! Don't leave the house today until you feel your very best. Stop hiding and start accentuating. At over 200 pounds I wore a bikini and posed before the mirror like a supermodel. I kept this up until I felt the presence of my sex goddess coming through me again.

Why does feeling good work? Because, like the workings of a magnet, when we feel good we draw to us more feel-good feelings. Appreciate who you are and you will notice appreciation all around you. You can do this. I love you. I believe in you. Begin today, right now. Appreciate one thing about yourself and then watch the appreciation grow. You are a sex goddess. Unleash your inner sex goddess and embrace a life full of energy, excitement, and fulfillment.

You have to be able to see yourself as gorgeous and sexy inside before you will experience sexiness in real time. You have to believe it is possible for you, because it very well is! Nothing can improve for you while you remain stuck in a state of disbelief. If you don't believe in the inner goddess, you will not work for her manifestation. Your energies will seep out and away from her fulfillment. You may be accustomed to feeling drab and unimpressed with yourself, maybe because you've accepted these attitudes from outside influences. Just because you've accepted something up to this point does not mean that you must continue living this way. Investigate new possibilities for yourself. You cannot reinvent your past, but you can direct your present in such a way that your future bespeaks health and power. See a new truth for yourself, one in which you are and have always been nurtured in the pursuit of your dreams. You don't need new parents to make this possible. You can be that support for yourself. Write yourself a new and empowering truth and live it!

Truth comes in many forms. Millions of opposing truths color our lives. You could have been born to a prostitute who in turn prostituted you out since childhood. In order to cope with such truths, you turned to drugs to numb the pain of reality. Your truth? Hopefully not, but it is someone's truth. It could become our truth if ever we chose it. We could choose to prostitute ourselves for drugs, and our truth would immediately be that we are drug-abusing prostitutes. My point is that there is a heavy amount of choice to the truth that falls into our area of Personal Power (Box One). Since this power of choice is under our control, we have the capacity to make optimal choices about who we will become.

Every one of us carries unlimited potential, but much of this power lies dormant because we don't really believe that the choice is ours whenever we are ready to improve ourselves. We look into the foggy past to define ourselves, which can be great if we had an awesome past. For those of us who have been beat up, put down, ridiculed, criticized, and taught self-shame, we can choose today to seek our higher selves. The world will do us no favors unless we get down to kicking in our walls of self-disbelief.

At one point you did believe in yourself. You once dreamed up big dreams, used your imagination to its fullest extent, and felt like you were really something special. And then the world took that from you. Maybe you allowed it; maybe you didn't have a choice. It doesn't matter because the results are all the same. If you're reading this, you have a choice right now. You can choose to believe in yourself and in your "silly" dreams. You can choose to eliminate the truths in your past that made you out to be less than you truly are. You do know who you are inside. My goal is to help you reclaim your power. You have the ability to turn your life into one that excites you and that challenges you to become more of your greatest self. Don't let the beautiful, wonderful, and sexy person inside you be swindled at the hands of the rest of the world's unbelief. As is most often the case, the naysayers matter little when it comes to you. If you allow others to rob you of a better life from this moment on, you are solely liable for the damages. This is to say, from now on it is your fault when you suffer.

As far as I or anyone knows, we get only one life to live. One life. Don't waste today while you wait until tomorrow to live as who you are meant to be. If you knew you had just one day left to live, you would make it count. Right? Consider the rest of your life to be your last day on Earth. Now are you ready to make it count?

God gives us a string of days to live until our time comes to leave this world. We all must die someday, yet we persist in living as if this will never happen to us. Surely we will be the one to live forever. I know that might not be what we're thinking or saying externally, but we are acting and living at least subconsciously as if death will never come to us. Death will come. What will you be able to say on that day? Will you look over your life and know you lived to your fullest soul expression? Or will you sit in regret like so many who allowed their essence to go with them to the grave? Refuse to do this to yourself. Make it a non-option in your life. Tell yourself the following:

> "I refuse to walk through life asleep. I will not let others dictate my life and define who I am. Instead, I will take charge of the things I control. I will make decisions that reflect who I am inside. I will live by what I believe after careful reflection and self-examination."

This is just too important to understate. Subtlety and sensitivity are for employee evaluations and pointing out bad breath. This is your life we are talking about. Your one and only! All I'm saying to you now is that you live out loud. Do not allow others to live it for you, to dictate their beliefs and interests to you. Define your beliefs in a way that honors who you are inside. If you do not know who you are inside, now is the time to find out. Now--not tomorrow or next month or on your next vacation from the job you hate--right now! Every day you fail to follow yourself severely increases the odds of you continuing to live only for and through others. You become a puppet of the media, or of your parents, or of your loved ones or children. Do you want the lives of others to run your own? Hopefully not. Oftentimes those you observe aren't living as they ought to be, either. If you meet that rare individual who is living in a fully actualized state, invite her in as a mentor. But always bear in mind that you are always the only expert on you. Once you accept that as your guiding truth, then you can build a deep and lasting relationship with yourself.

And quit dismissing your own better judgment and gut instincts that others want to negate. Quit replacing your intuitive voice with the demands of others. No more! I believe in you, but I matter about as much as those people who doubt you. You and you alone have to believe in you. Period. You need you on your side. So get in the game and start playing. And above all, have fun!

Final Thoughts

Becoming Love

It is your responsibility to add love to the world by becoming love yourself. Love who you are. Love who others are. Love what the world *is*. Refuse to place stipulations on love, as if one had to improve in order to earn love's power.

When you take a self-inventory, do you find yourself filled with love and peace, or are you perhaps depleted by anger and exhaustion? If you find the latter, demand that you give yourself a fuller life. Hold yourself accountable to make better and more love-filled choices. Decide to process your past by cleaning up your messy addictions. Make it a priority to heal every wounded part of your past.

Forgiveness is the active expression of love. It is the magic cure for resentment and bitterness. You may argue that some people just aren't worthy of forgiveness. Maybe even you can't forgive your own self. What about people who aren't sorry for what they've done? Why should we ever forgive them? The answer is simple but often difficult to truly grasp. It's not about them anyway!

Finding freedom from your bitterness toward the bad actions of others is not about forcing them to become better people. If you intend on waiting for them to reform before you offer forgiveness, you may wait until the end of time. The pain inside you, the violation and your utter devastation over what others have done to you, is not about them anymore. They were the tornado that ripped through your home, but it is up to you to pick up the pieces. The tornado will never come back and offer an apology or reform into a kinder, gentler cloud formation. The person who hurt you doesn't have to be present or even alive on this earth for you to forgive what they've done to you. This does not mean you accept the person back into your life. Instead, you let go of the pain they caused you.

Forgiveness isn't holding on; it's letting go. It is you saying, "I release the pain that I've been carrying around all this time." Too many of us hold onto our anger and defensiveness as a protective shield against further harm. The problem is that this shield does not let in love or peace. It blocks anything good from getting into your heart center. This can be a temporary coping mechanism, but over time it blocks you from experiencing the deep ecstasies of life. You cut yourself off from good. Own that. Own the areas where you, not anyone else, hold onto past hurts and cut yourself off from the positive flow of the future. Own the times when you were bitter when you could have been happy, angry when you could have been excited, exhausted instead of filled with love. Own your personal pitfalls and really get how it has always been you blocking yourself from happiness's flow.

Too many of us have giant messes inside ourselves that we've put off cleaning for far too long. Much of it was dumped there through outside influences, but we've kept ourselves down. We can feel overwhelmed quickly when we take stock of it all. No wonder many of us continue feeling burdened by emotions without really knowing why. We feel angry or depressed long after the events have passed that had once made us feel justified in our anger or depression. Checking how your energies are arranged in your Grid helps you to sort your inner treasures from your inner trash heap. Get rid of whatever keeps your treasure hidden beneath the rubble of old pains and personal grudges.

Give back to yourself through the art of forgiveness, regardless of what others think of you. Forgiveness means giving back to others what they tried to make you feel, and you can do the same with yourself. Get rid of what you no longer want about yourself. Eliminate the garbage you've buried yourself under. The process begins and ends with you. If you remain angry and bitter, the world will remember you only for that. Realize once and for all that forgiveness means releasing every wrong you've done to others and to yourself.

I realize that some acts are far more difficult to forgive than others. I'm here to tell you that you must find a way to release your energies from remaining pent up inside the External Stressors of Box Two. I believe in you. You can free yourself from the chains of grudges twisting around your soul. Only you can say what your path to healing will be. It may be as simple as making a decision now and forever to stop being held captive by the chains of the past. You will never know for sure until you take the steps toward healing. I'm merely here as your guide to point you in the direction of healing and to emphasize its value in transforming you into a more authentic creation. The work is up to you. No one in the world will ever be able to reach into your energetic Grid and "fix" you. Support helps, to be sure, but only when you open yourself to help.

Be the support you are missing in your life. Return all the old pains that you've let weigh you down for too long now. If you feel it is beyond your capacity to forgive completely at this time, ask your higher power on your behalf. This is a major step in the right direction, and it is enough until you are ready to forgive totally on your own.

The ultimate goal throughout all the energetic observation and cleansing work of this book is to return you to a present moment filled with peace, love, and joy. We address the past only so we can clear through it and clean it up. Follow the wisdom of the Cherokee proverb that teaches, "Don't let yesterday use up too much of today."

Remember that it is never about them. Healing and release is always within you. Do this not for your family, your friends, your enemies, or even for me. Do it for yourself simply because you are worth it. The gift of you is the best present you could ever give to anyone in your world. The people in your life want you! We all want to see you. Refuse to play the victim in your inner prison, and step into the light of your whole self.

Be the example of a darkened life come into the light. We need more beacons in this world to point the way for all spiritual pilgrims who aspire to a better life. Spread love by becoming love. People around you will know you as a love light when they feel your presence in the room. They will respond, sometimes subconsciously, by radiating more love themselves. Becoming an example of love's power to heal the wounds of the past is the finest gift you can offer to the world. From where I'm sitting, becoming love is the only way to achieve total absolution from the past and to remain a light for generations who will follow your example.

Blessings.

CPSIA information can be obtained at www.ICGtesting.com
Printed in the USA
BVOW030313070213

312603BV00002B/31/P

9 781452 560779

The Father's Hand

A collection of Poems
By John Mansfield

A Word from John's Wife Ann

John was born in Lowestoft in 1931 and was taken home by the Lord whilst living in Carmarthen in 2018. He was a beloved husband, father, grandfather and friend, and is deeply missed.

There aren't enough words to sufficiently describe John, but here are a few. He was unceasingly kind, caring, loving and, most of all, humble. His formula for life was 'just believe'. He loved the Lord greatly and it gave him enormous pleasure to write poems for and about his wonderful Saviour. It would make his heart sing to know that he is able to share these with you now.

God Bless

Ann

ISBN 9798363713569

Text Copyright © David John Mansfield 2022
Illustrations Copyright © Carol M Weir 2022

Compiled by Hazel Wilcox. For more information please email gazzwil41@yahoo.co.uk

All rights reserved. No part of this book may be used or reproduced in any form or by any means, electrical or mechanical, including photocopying, scanning, recording, taping or by information storage and retrieval system without the permission of the author and/or illustrator.

Contents

Chapter 1:   Praise and Worship
Chapter 2:   The Return of the Lord
Chapter 3:   Christmas
Chapter 4:   Creation
Chapter 5;   The Holy Scriptures
Chapter 6:   Salvation
Chapter 7:   Easter
Chapter 8:   Prayer
Chapter 9:   The Holy Spirit
Chapter 10:   Love
Chapter 11:   Heaven
Chapter 12:   Protection

Index of Illustrations

1. URC Praise and Worship
2. Jesus in the Clouds
3. Bethlehem Stable Scene
4. Vertical Sunset, Morecambe Bay
5. Sunset, Bible, Sword and Crown
6. Bridge at Riversley Park
7. Jesus Breaking Bread and Wine Goblet
8. Manuscript and Praying Hands
9. Sunset, Clouds and Doves
10. Jesus Knocking at the Door
11. Forest Stream
12. Bird Statue by the Platform

Cover Illustration:
Low Tide at Sunderland Point

Other works by this artist can be found on the Facebook Page 'Carol Mary Weir'

The Father's Hand

The waves of the sea that wash the shore
And keep its pebbles clean
Is liken to the land we plough
It is cleansed by hands unseen

We plant the seed from harvest past
And it rests in fertile land
Until the time of season comes
Then is touched by God's own hand

The shoots of green, the infant corn
Comes proudly from the land
And points its head heavenward
In thanks to the Father's hand

The corn grows tall and does not fall
Held firmly by its roots
Until it's growing days are done
Until it bears its fruit

Joy and peace is what You bring
With the harvest of our soul
And daily bread is what You bring
When you crown the corn of gold

We thank you, Lord, on this harvest day
For Your gifts of bread on table lay
We cannot live on bread alone
But it feeds the body until it's coming home

We give praise to You, our loving God
For the table you have graced
For through the wonders of Your hand
We see our Saviour's face

Humbly Yours

Oh Lord, what praise can I give
Only from this humble heart
But even these small words I give
Are all I have, that are from the heart

For those words grow strong in power
When we practice what we say
And give to You each precious hour
Our love each blessed day

For, oh Lord, there is a place
Where all these words may grow
It is the love within my heart
For, my God, I love You so

Truth

The voice that comes upon my heart
The sound that opens up my ears
The light that makes my heart to see
It is your hand that is teaching me

Your hand that made the smallest flower
And did paint the fields around it
Is the hand that touched my heart
And paints the joy that fills it

There is no greater artist, Lord
Than you that paints the heavens
The beauty of the rising sun
And the glory of its setting

You, my Lord, paint heaven and earth
With a hand that is so loving
And into those hands we give our all
Secure with the Father's blessings

Praise

Let all our voices praise as one
When to our Lord in praise we come
And may our souls unite together
To bring your praise, my
Lord, forever

And when you come in all Your glory
A trumpet blast will part the sky
Then begins the endless story
And we will dwell with You on high

So, great Lord of all creation
The God of love that comes for me
You are the God of every nation
We will, as one, give praise to Thee

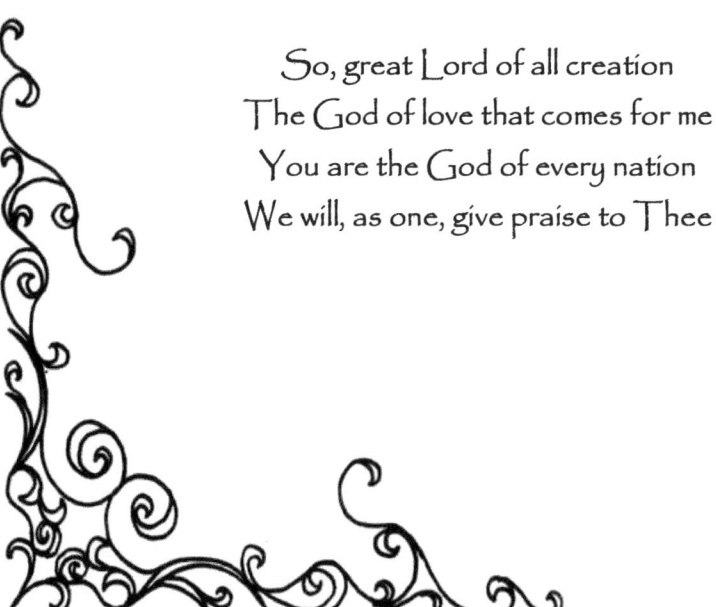

The Glory of our King

I praise the glory of our King
The King that formed creation
I praise His majesty, and sing
My songs of adoration

He is the father of my soul
His days have no ending
The glorious path He has prepared
Is beneath my feet unbending

Therefore, I praise the Shepherd King
And pray that I may pasture
In His flock on heaven's road
And graze there ever after

The sound I hear along the way
Are bells of joy and rapture
For the Lord has taken His children
Where Satan cannot capture

Praise – Repentance and Life Anew

My God, you are the one that comforts me
You are the blessing my soul can see
The rock of my salvation
When shadows cover the nation

The light you bring, that melts the mist
The hand you bring with closed tight fist
Opens the skies to heaven
To destroy our sins forever

Your voice that is so sweet of sound
It flows into our clouded minds
Fills our hearts with pleasure
And fills them with godly measure

Hear the voice of our heavenly king
As to our hearts great joy He brings
He will take away our fears
He is our God that really cares

Jesus, though my heart is stained
Your love for me will never change
Yes, by that stain made by my sin
Still you open the door and let me in

Oh gracious Lord, merciful Saviour
Forgive my sins and my behaviour
May your peace descend on me
And by faith set me free

Our blessed hope – to dwell with you
Is the hope in our life renewed
Born again into Your fold
Will give us the truth on which to hold

The sins I had that conquered me
Are the sins that nailed you to that tree
I am not worthy of Your sacrifice
But you died, and paid my life changing price

Lord, when I talk to you

Lord, the tongue I use when to you I speak
Is fed by the Holy Spirit
If it sounds humble and meek
It is the voice of the Holy Spirit

For He teaches me with pleasing tongue
To worship and praise my Lord
He shows me how His praise is sung
And his grace on me is poured

When I feel the pulling of my heart
And I know that God is there
I feel the sin and dark depart
Then my thought becomes a prayer

From the peace that comes to me
There grows a fruitful vine
It is a fresh new life I see
And a taste of heaven's wine

Jesus became the way of life
My past was a fading dream
And all my sins and woes and strife
Had gone, by sacrifice supreme

When He Comes

When the clouds divide to reveal your throne
Let not this earthly life draw us home
For a blink of the eye is too short by far
Lord, my true home is waiting where you are

The coat you leave in harvest field
Has no value when Jesus reveals
The glory of His coming again
To take us home from Satan's pain

We know not when that hour will come
We know not when God will blacken the sun
We know not when the moon grows dim
But we know it will come, because of Him

Have faith you Christians, watch the sky
And know in Christ you never die
When He wakes you with his trumpet call
Be ready my friend, lest you may fall

Your home in heaven with our Father's Son
To dwell with Him, the day will come
But there is no greater place to be
Clothed in God's glory, His beauty to see

The Coming Storm

The coming storm is gathering now
The time for sinners to hide or bow
For the Christ who comes from heavenly throne
Is coming to take His children home

His glory will sweep the mighty sky
And the blast of the trumpet will be the cry
To children saved from Satan's tomb
Hear the voice of Jesus,
"come home ~ come home"

Children of our heavenly King
To you that day new life will bring
He knows what sins are in our hearts
So cleanse them now, before it starts

Be ready for that glorious day
And let your prayers be true ~ and say
"Excite my heart ~ excite my soul
And let Your love in me unfold"

For at the time when You appear
To be with You ~ I have no fear
But if You wash me clean of sin
My fight against evil I will surely win

And so by the blood of the precious Lamb
I will hear the call of the great "I AM"
And I will surely know my way is steady
So Lord Jesus come, for I am ready

The Vision

I see before me a window small
I see the future, I see it all
I see where God's hand has left the land
The desolation and abomination of man's own hand

The window I see is the final scene
Strong men faint where evil has been
Tribulation from which one cannot hide
Has begun with terror and blood where the church has died

I see through a window, for in my wake
I am with Jesus, by the rapture's sake
I am so thankful to be in this heavenly place
Than to be below where all is terror and waste

Our choice in life is easy to make
But the future it brings is hard to take
If our choice is God's heavenly place
We can't forget the horrors in that evil waste

Before time strikes and angels sing
Be sure your path is Jesus our King
For down below in fiery hell
You fall alone, no tale to tell

Lord, You fill my Heart

Lord, You fill my heart with love and grace
You showed me where to end the race
But time is not important here
For the race will finish when You appear

You will come, Lord Jesus, mine
For the prophetic events are on the vine
And the fruit of the vine is ripened at last
And the harvest of your church is about to pass

Even so, come Lord Jesus

The Rapture

There is a greatness in the air
A majestic expectancy is nigh
The coming of Jesus is very near
When his glory will fill the sky

Nothing on earth can stop our Lord
No power, no politician
For He will come at God's command
To take His church to heaven

All our worship we will give
To our Lord who comes to take us
For He will come, as His children pray
Come ~ come Lord Jesus

Christmas

The Voice of Christmas

I hear a voice on Christmas Day
Calling all people on earth to pray
To thank our God for his only Son
Born to us 'The Blessed One'

From that cradle, a humble stall
Came the voice of a babe, a joyful call
He is the Spirit that we might live
The Spirit that he would freely give

This child who on manger lay
Was born on humble cattle hay
This lowly back door where He came in
Was the way to see the darkest sin

Mystery filled the earth that day
Wise men from the eastern way
Shepherds coming to His cradle stall
The place where the heavenly star did fall

Children know this sweet child's name
But not all men would be the same
For wrong is measured in this world of sin
So God's light in Jesus has souls to win

So raise your voice this glorious day
And praise that babe on manger hay
From humble birth He did proclaim
I am the way – the truth – God's burning flame

Lord as we celebrate Your Son's birth
Let us feast with joy and mirth
For Jesus, our Saviour, Son of our King
Is born that He our salvation brings

The Light Has Come

On that night – that glorious night
Our God gave us new birth
For here the Prince of Glory lay
The Saviour of this earth

God gave His Son to a world so dark
To bring light to the hearts of men
For man was stumbling in the dark
Void of a shepherd to tend

Lord you gave us a Saviour boy
The fruit He bore with love and joy
His hands that clutch at mother's shawl
Were the hands that are creation's call

The hands that bless the poor and needy
The hands that healed the sick and greedy
The hands that restored that life that failed
The hands that bore the sinner's nail

So the baby born on humble hay
Was the Son of God born that day
Born to build salvation's path
To take us from our sinful past

This was the night – a special night
This was a night so clear
For from a cold dark stable stall
Came a voice the world would hear

The air was still and quiet that night
And shepherds heard the call
As angels filled the heavenly sky
And pointed to the stall

May the sound of angel wings
Fall gently round our hearts
And lift our praise, Oh Lord, to you
That we may never part

All glory to Almighty King
To us this Christmastide did bring
The infant Jesus – Lord of all
Crowned upon that humble stall

Lord Jesus bring to mind this day
The memory of your birth
And let the nations praise You Lord
Every nation upon this earth

Amen

Behold the Christ Child

A star that was so big and bright
Appeared to all that glorious night
And neath the brilliance of its light
The child of God is born, pure white

All around the heavens sang
To hail the dawn of God's own Lamb
For on that hay all life did lay
A shepherd to guide and show the way

For here on lowly stable stall
Lay the head that is creation's call
For sin was rife upon God's earth
So his Son He gave to give new birth

We should know the sacrifice
That God has made to give us life
He knew the trials His Son would face
To purchase souls from sinful taste

All glory to our God and King
His loving Son to us doth bring
The Saviour of this world is born
And we should praise this blessed morn

Shepherds

To us this blessed day is born
A Saviour on bed of hay
Although He brought a wondrous light
The world was not ready to begin the fight

The shepherds saw a wonderful sight
Afraid, but full of joy
They saw the sky ablaze with light
Of angels praising God's Christ boy

The Shepherds came to worship He
That the angels opened the way to see
They knelt before humble stall
To worship the King who is Lord of all

Wondrous night, wondrous light
The King of Kings is born
Only a babe at mothers breast
But already great hopes are formed

This glorious child so meek and mild
God's offspring, God's own Son
Is come to light in this dark, dark world
And put Satan on the run

Fill your heart with joyous praise
For tonight the world will see
The long-awaited Saviour Boy
From crib to Calvary

May the power and peace of this baby boy
Be yours to have and hold
And may this night lift your heart
And the wonders of God untold

Christmas

I fall upon my knees this morn
And cry out in wonder this glorious dawn
As all the angels in heaven sing
When to the earth His Son He brings

Thank you, Lord, for this coming day
As for your Son, we earnestly pray
He has come, this mighty King
And by His love, salvation brings

He is the author of all that's good
And under his arm He carries a book
And before the veil is open to me
I pray my name in His book I see

God's New Day

Behold, the dawn melts the evening sky
All shadows are made to fly
To make way for the rising sun
The coming day has just begun

In fertile fields and forest green
God's hand will change the evening scene
The rising sun will cast its beams
Upon the earth, where night has been

Heralding birds will welcome the dawn
God gave them the song for the new day born
God's carpet of gold where the wildflowers grow
Hurries down to the stream and drinks from its flow

Each day the earth freshens it's face
Each day God adorns it with His grace
And changes from old to new
And bathes it with gentle dew

His hands are full of love to give
Let his blessing show the way to live
Open them with a prayer
That he can show his loving care

Creation

The great creation that has no match
And our God that made it all
Formed the egg that it should hatch
And gave life to this barren ball

The ball that turned in endless sky
Became the world we know
A place of beauty that will never die
A place where life can grow

The creator God of that living ball
Gave us a choice to grow
A choice to follow his loving call
Or make roads to the hell below

Creation is a mighty thing
And it's awesome to our minds
But greater is the God that brings
Those wonders of great design

When earthly disaster happens to man
When distress grieves his heart
He turns to God and blames His hand
And asks why he allowed it to start (Cont'd)

If your house is destroyed by raging storms
And your life is desolation
Does God tell you to rebuild again
Upon the same foundation

Did God tell us to build upon sand
Or to build on solid rock
It is our choice, the choice of man
Where to raise our flock

If you ask the Lord to guide your way
Then rock would be his reply
For He is the rock where foundation lay
For upon God we can rely

God made this world to please man
And for man to please our God
But are we thankful for the land
And the wealth on which we trod

Around us beauty carpets the hills
The stars cling to the sky
The streams and brooks that ripple
Sound like a lover's sigh

Oh wondrous God who made all things
We thank you for this dream
And we know that when heaven comes
It will surpass all our eyes have ever seen

Lord, every eye will turn to You
Every knee shall bow
And every treasure of Christ our King
Will soothe our heavy brow

If Jesus lives within your heart
You have been promised a blessed hope
Then our bonds with Christ will never part
With love – the bonding rope

For I know the rock to which I cling
Is You, Lord Jesus, my heavenly King
The rock that bears the life I seek
Is refuge to the humble and the meek

Your creation grants us wondrous things
Whatever scene you see
But nothing compares to the heaven you bring
The blessed hope that will surely be

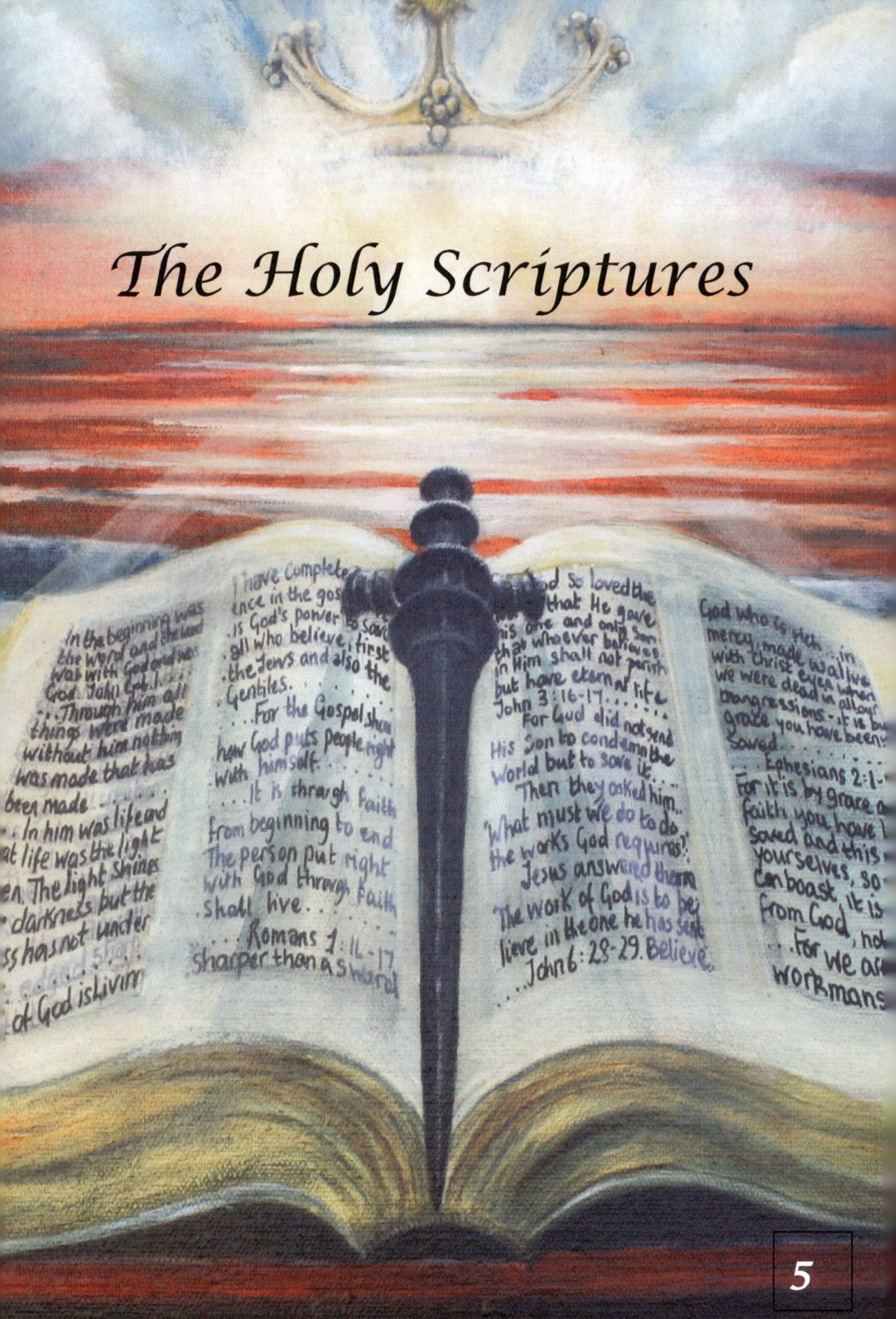

The Power of God's Word

Come into my heart, oh Lord of mine
Fill me with Your very kind
Let the flood that enters me
Cleanse my soul, Your love to see

For though my heart is filled with joy
I must release its essence
To show my brothers how it feels
To know Your glorious presence

For through my eyes of wonderment
Your wondrous works I see
And like a mirror they reflect
Your word and your kingdom's key

Eternal Rest

When life on this earth is done
When all pain and strife has gone
When worry and fear has been met
Our Spirit of God will no longer fret
Because we know we will be with the Lord
Of this we have been greatly assured
By God's Word in His heavenly book
Which by faith we followed and undertook
We did our best to follow His Son
We will walk in His footsteps while this race is run
And now at the close of this earthly day
We hope to hear our Saviour say
Enter my friend, you did your best
Enter my heaven for your eternal rest

Lord Lead Us

Lord, lead us in Your footsteps true
They take us safely home to You
The glory of our living God
Is in every step our feet have trod
And the majesty of Jesus Christ
Is on this road of Christian life

The peace that comes to fill your heart
Comes from our Lord from the very start
But on this road you must obey
The blessed word the Lord will say
For every word comes from God above
And the greatest of his words is LOVE

Born Again

I do not seek the praise of man
I come to God just as I am
I seek only the living Word
That my faith has gently stirred

The Word – the message that comes from God
Is joy upon my ears
It brings new life and rebirth
It heals the sinful years

For when His Word has touched us
With hands that are bloodied too
He knew the hurt we suffered
For He had suffered to

The pains He suffered were healing pains
That healed our wounded souls
With healing that leaves no scar
Of past sins – not retold

Be born again from above
And let our life begin
For there is no other life
That can be free from sin

Saved

You came to me, oh Lord my God
And snatched me from the mire
You washed me clean by blood so pure
And dressed me in Your desire

So by the grace You have given me
And by the love we share
Plant in me a life to grow
From gutter to saint - a crown to wear

Jesus came into my life
Through door that was open wide
He filled my heart with a light
That grew brighter by His side

I know my love grows stronger
When walking in His stride
I live now by the Church of God
Waiting for it's bride

There will come that glorious day
When trumpet fills the sky
And You Lord Jesus will come at last
To claim your faithful bride

The Coming Light

Lord, You take away my sceptre
And give me a crown of gold
When I follow in Your footsteps
To a land that is foretold

Lord, many hearts have seen your signs
And many souls are saved
But many still walk behind
And are close to an eternal grave

I pray, oh Lord, for those lost sheep
For the ones that stray behind
And trust that You will find and keep
Those of stubborn mind

I pray, oh Lord, that they may see
The truth beyond the grave
And that the light of our living God
Will show their way, and save

Oh God, our Father and Heavenly King
To You our praise and worship bring
You give us, Lord, joy untold
And lead us to your heavenly fold

You found me, Lord

Oh Lord that has given me life anew
Fill my heart with joy for You
Take me to the boundaries of love
And open the way to your heaven above

For in your hands I feel no shame
Of my past life where morals were lame
Where darkness was the life I made
Then your light closed wounds as darkness fade

Heal these wounds by Your love and care
And let my sins forever die in fear
For now Your light that shines in me
Will close these wounds and set me free

Your son, my God, took souls from hell
As my soul can witness with tales to tell
Of deaths where there was nowhere to go
Jesus came there and rescued my soul

Loving father who hears my prayer
I pray that You my thanks will hear
A thank You that is greater than words
A trophy I am to Your greatness and worth

Straining Forward

For on the way that lay head
Do not look behind
It is laid by the blood our Lord had shed
When he closed the gates of time

The time of past and sinful years
That wrapped our souls in pain
And all the darkness and the fears
Are gone by the light we gain

May we then praise our heavenly Lord
And worship His holy name
Let us walk that path ahead
And heed not from where He came

Set Me Free

Lord, take away the evil shroud
That covers my sinful heart
Cast out the author of that cloud
That my sins may then depart

And may the glory of Your love
Always shine on me
And by Your loving touch, my Lord
Burst the chains and set me free

For the very soul I have is yearning
To meet it's Lord once again
My very heart is fiercely burning
To see my Jesus – to be free again

So when at last the pain is gone
I will see Your glorious face
When through life's veil I finally come
I know that heaven is in this place

Sin is Evil

Sin is evil, sin is death
Sin will take away your breath
Lord, sin will close Your open door
And we will see Your light no more

Death is like a creeping sore
It will eat the flesh to its deepest core
Our body feels good when we do our will
But sin festers inside and will finally kill

So treat your body with the balm of God
And lift your hearts from it's comfort pod
Open the way to God's glorious Son
The healing then has begun

For by His Word and His faithful love
His hand will be ready from above
To take repentance from your heart
And give your life a God filled start

Jesus Christ will show the way
The debt of your sins He will lovingly pay
That is why He suffered on the cross
To take your sins and bury the dross

So lift your sins to God and say
"Forgive me Lord, I earnestly pray
For now I give to You my heart
And by Your grace give life a new start"

New Life

When suddenly the garden bare
Became a flowering sensation
For God had touched the barren soil
And formed a new creation

Like my soul, oh Lord my God
You touched me with your love
And made me humble to serve you, Lord
By blessings from above

You gave me new creation
By the miracle of rebirth
You filled my heart with joy and peace
And treasure of boundless worth

Oh Lord, your very name I breathe
With a mind so full of grace
And a heart that beats with every word
I see in my Saviour's face

The Race

The race in which I now take part
Is not for the glory of my heart
But for the one who gave me fame
To take the race in His glorious name

His spirit in these legs that run
Will take me on till the race is won
Then my Lord will say to me
Well done my child, there is no fee

For in this race there is no cost
It was paid by Jesus on the cross
He took away the sins of mine
And took me over the winning line

Come Lord Jesus

The Lord and Saviour of mankind
Help us pray, Your love to find
Help us to know Your perfect way
That we are ready, on that glorious day

When you come, Jesus, Lord of mine
To hear Your call, "My child, it's time"
It's then I will know my path is true
The one I chose to follow You

It's then I knew I had no life
I gave it to You upon Your sacrifice
And as You entered my troubled heart
You took my sins and tore them apart

You planted then a life in me
This was the life to set me free
So now with simple heart renewed
I see only the way to follow You

So, come Lord Jesus, I hear your call
There is no dark, I cannot fall
So open your arms and take me in
This soul that once was wracked with sin

The one that gave His life for me
When He was nailed upon that tree
He's waiting on the clouds on high
And His time is coming to call us nigh

Your Will Be Done

I seek not Your crowns for pleasure
But only to know I have done Your will
I seek not Your power for pleasure
But only to know I have
climbed that hill

For in the darkened days behind me
I knew such terror in delight
I saw that hill surrounded by evil
Until I saw Your saving light

For the path that was shrouded
with evil
Is now filled with love and light
But I have found my Lord and saviour
Through the darkest of the night

Prayer of Conversion

Lord, I came to You with a sinful heart
A heart that was made of stone
I came to You with a heavy heart
A heart that had no soul

You heard my cry call out to You
You heard a hollow sound
That sound of dark despair You knew
And you turned that prayer around

For by Your mercy and wondrous grace
You restored my soul to live
You filled the hollow sounds with glorious taste
Of freedom from sin, so my soul to You I give

Now, from the shadows of evil way
I come into God's light
Before me the path that Jesus lay
Where He is centred with majesty and might

The Door Through the Cross

Through the cross we sinners came
To face the Christian way
To follow Jesus the risen Christ
And live in His glorious name

Any other way is certain death
For we lose heaven's call
And follow the other slippery path
Where in Satan's net we fall

Jesus opened the door through the cross
Where we sinners became renewed
He had taken the sins we lost
And gave us life anew

He hung up on that cross
Suffering our cruel pain
So we could enter through the door
Free from the burden He claimed

So on Easter morn we celebrate
Not for the worldly things
But for the way from the cross
To the place where Jesus is King

The Heavy Door

I know not where the roses go
But only the scent they leave
I know not where my life has gone
But only the times I grieve

I know the wonders of God's hand
I see them every day
But have I seen the shifting sands
That opened the Saviour's Way

When Jesus called me to His side
When I opened that heavy door
Was my body prepared to die
And see my sins no more

Then the spirit of God came in
Through that heavy door
And washed away my earthly sin
And God saw that sin no more

I praise my God for that unforgettable day
When his Son I found at last
And I thank Him for the debt He paid
On that simple, magnificent cross

The New Dawn

The sun that rises in the new morning sky
Stretches out it's fingers of light
These fingers seek the darkest place
To give it glorious light

The hearts and souls of darkened minds
The minds that get no sleep
Are led and fed by Satan's kind
And stumble in darkest deep

But if they seek the light that comes
Those of darkened minds
They will find that morning sun
And are fed by God's own kind

A kind that will give them bread of life
A life of light secure
A life that will give them joy and peace
And a hope of heaven so pure

So trample upon that life of sin
Open your hearts and let God in
And may that finger of morning light
Point your way and give you sight

God that gives you glorious light
And Jesus his Son, a star so bright
Will conquer Satan that took your soul
And win it back by love untold

I Met A Stranger

As I walked along a distant shore
I saw a stranger I had seen before
As He drew near, I could see so clear
The nature of this man so fair

His face was like the shining stars
On His body were the nail made scars
He beckoned me to follow Him
He spoke and said "Release your sins"

I cried out "You are the man
The one who was sent by the great I AM
They said You would take my sins away
If I would kneel before You and pray"

"Jesus is your name," I said
"I could place my sins where You had bled
For You had bled that I may be
A new creation for Your heaven to see"

The man I met upon the beach that day
Had said "If you want me I'm here to stay
For there is no truth, but to come to me
I will feed you for all eternity"

Door to the Blessed Hope

I opened the door to your knock
And the door became a solid rock
That it may not move or close again
That Jesus would always stay and reign

Come in, my Saviour, the door is wide
Flood through the gates like endless tide
I welcome You with heart and soul
To dine with me and cast the mould

The darkness that filled my eyes that day
When I opened the door and asked Him to stay
Were suddenly filled with dazzling light
As Jesus gave these eyes new sight

He took my sin that gave wretched life
They hung with Him upon the cross of strife
And from His suffering and His pain
My faith and love for Him was gained

This life that came to me that day
Was unbelievable, no words can say
This came from the touch of my Lord's hand
And his blessings poured like finest sand

So praise we give You day by day
To come to You by prayer we pray
From the treasures of my joy filled heart
Comes love that binds and never parts

The Holy Scar

There is a scar upon that hill
where they crucified my Lord
The scar was black and turned to red
when they crucified my Lord

There was a scar upon my soul
Where sin had wounded me
But as His blood ran down that hill
It washed and set me free

When I was in the darkest place
I had fallen there in despair
When I came to that darkest hour
Jesus was waiting there

The earthly things that form this life
My eyes are weary of
For now my spirit has new height
And sees the truth and God

In the radiance of His light
My soul becomes secure
And in the love that comes by faith
We see our Saviour pure

So Lord, the scar up on that hill
Has a beauty of its own
And the blood that fell upon that hill
Became a crown of gold

A thousand faces pass me by
But only one I see
The face of my Lord Jesus Christ
The one that died for me

He died upon that dreadful cross
And made that scar of old
But I would rather suffer all loss
To gain that crown of gold

An Easter Message

Above the earth a cross was raised
And on its form – our Lord was nailed
He suffered that our souls be saved
So that the Lord – our Christ – be hailed

For in that time of agony
My Lord did suffer – just for me
That His blood may wash my sin
And open the door to let Him in

Oh blessed Saviour of mankind
Who came from heaven to sinful earth
That we would know a godly mind
And live with Him in new birth

For on the resurrection day
The fear of death has passed away
In Jesus – death is just a veil
When lifted – reveals the eternal way

When I see the Cross

Lord, when I see the cross on which You died
I can hardly breathe, for I could not hide
You suffered there for sins I bore
Not Yours, but mine, you suffered for

Lord, if I could start my life again
I would see your redeeming pain
I would see you suffer there
I would open my heart to your loving care

But now it is done, you suffered and died
Suddenly my sins could not hide
They had gone; YOU had taken them, not to keep
But had cast them, forgotten, into oceans deep

And now the life my heart yearned for
Has come to me through Your open door
It was always there for me to see
It was Your crucified body that saved me

The Sacrifice

The light faded around His head
As He hung there in our shame
The life He gave and blood He shed
Was ailing when he called his Father's name
The thorns upon His holy brow
Stung with searing pain
The nails driven through His holy flesh
Entered the cross of shame

"My Father, forgive these heartless men
That nailed me to this tree
And may the guilt not fall on them
But help to set them free
My mission on earth is closing now
I have completed my Father's task
The light I brought to sinful earth
Has filled the sinner's cask"

This earthly life is now diminished
His sorrow he could not hide
In dying voice He said 'It is finished'
Then He bowed His head and died
What thoughts have we of brutal pain
How can we know, was it all in vain
Or did those nails pierce our heart too
It was, you know, for me and you

If you feel His love and terrible pain
And it was your sins He suffered for
Then you will know it was not in vain
For your salvation was the burden He bore
Now Lord our hearts are filled with joy
For we know what is to come
That glorious resurrection day
Your kingdom and Your reigning Son

Prayer and the Cross

As I kneel upon the ground I walk
My heart, through my tongue, begins to talk
From the darkness of my soul, a guiding light I behold
A light of truth that did unfold

The light of God I could not see
Until through prayer I found the key
A key to open the door from sin
Through prayer God opened his door and let me in

I found the way through simple prayer
The invisible God, did suddenly appear
My heart had turned from sour to gold
When committed, I heard that voice of old

Through the darkness a light had come
It melted the sin, my heart was won
My soul began to turn away
From the evil one, on that glorious day

My Lord, You have cleansed me clean
You raised the cross where sin had been
Through the cross I found my Lord
By His free love, I could never afford

Gracious God, how can it be
That the love You give is completely free
My debts were endless, You paid them too
By prayer and the cross You gave me life anew

Prayer and Faith

When we come to You in prayer
Lord, our Heavenly Father
We come with empty hearts to bare
The fruits of Your love within us

Help me Lord in my life for You
To follow your footsteps straight and true
To find at last in the things I do
Will take me to my home with You

But in this world of hate and fear
I hold my faith in You so dear
So Jesus, when Your voice I hear
Will help me with this life to bear

For in our faith in You our Lord
We know the day is nearing
When we will hear Your trumpet call
And the sight of You appearing

Help is in a Prayer

When your life is hard and day is done
When all seems lost and your eyes grow dim
Pray to the Lord and He will come
Look to the Lord and pray to Him

When you seem to have lost the fight
And you need a true, true friend
Then pray and you will see His light
Then He your troubles will mend

So pray to Jesus and the life you have
Will suddenly go right
And peace and love will come to you
As you walk within His light

What joy your heart will carry
What peace the Lord will send
What love you will have for everyone
With Jesus as your friend

Forgive Me

When morning prayer has passed away
It stays with God throughout the day
And when the day, it's time has run
My prayer returns with the setting sun

Morning and evening I seem to pray
Yet the blessings of God fill the day
For praising God, I must know
And thank Him as the day will go

Lord, You know every step I take
You see my ways and each mistake
You open the door before my eye
But my life is too busy, and I pass it by

I see others fall, and think "I'm fine"
I know my God, for with Him I dine
But to dine with Him is not enough
It's the reason I dine that I rebuff

For all my ways and all my talk
I still have not that saintly walk
Through the day, the things I do
I will say "God won't mind" but is that true

Our God hurts at every wrong I do
And I say "forgive me" and think that will do
To ask forgiveness takes our pain away
But do we ask our God to stay

To truly thank and please my God
And feel the comfort of His rod
I will pray to Him each and every day
And pray to Him all along my way

Now, I love His Son, who gave me new birth
And my prayers to Him must always be first
For I love His Son and follow His way
His kingdom will come on that final day

God Is But A Prayer Away

In the tents of the righteous I bring my lamp
That they may see and hear
In the fields of the righteous where they camp
I bring a harvest for all to share

I know my children by their hearts
And not the words I hear
When from their lips their prayer may part
Be sure it is a heartfelt prayer

A loyal prayer is a royal prayer
For our God is the King of Kings
So when you pray know He is near
Your heart will feel the joy He brings

For prayer takes away troubles and strife
And answers all our needs
They make level the roads of troubled life
And give life to His growing seed

Put your hands together and pray this day
Give meaning to the life you lead
Know that Jesus is the only way
For in His fold you will always feed

The Power of Prayer

When in depth I pray, my Lord
My heart becomes a fire
It devours the evil that is stored
And crushes Satan's power

In strength of prayer nothing stands
That is against the Lord
For in that prayer is great power
When we know that Christ is Lord

For at the opening of that door
We let our Saviour in
And when we are born again
He sees not where we have been

The Holy Spirit

Grace

Grace is not which comes and goes
It's not a passing dream
It is the Spirit of our God
That comes by hand unseen

The family that truly lives with God
Are blessed by his loving grace
They bond together like melted gold
And show our Saviour's face

When we meet Him face to face
We know we stand by His Spirit of grace
For had that mysterious power not been
This would have been a different scene

Your blessings come from heaven above
They come to us with wondrous love
They feed our bodies minds and soul
With grace, a treasure of finest gold

We leap upon the wings of God
He carries us to our home
And by the very grace of God
We foil the Satan's doom

You heal me Lord, when I fall down
You take the fall as I strike the ground
You raise me up and straighten my way
You walk with me where dangers lay

Plucked from despair, saved by his care
My soul is turned to gold
For now my way sees no fear
I have His hand to hold

His grace is a saving grace
It moulds our life to His
It places our hearts in His embrace
And fills us with heavenly bliss

Remember that the life you live
Is truly shown by the love you give

Joy in my Heart

There is a joy within my heart
A joy that I can keep
A joy that grows and never parts
A joy whose roots are deep

The joy that is God's own Son
Whose love doth comfort me
A joy that is set and does not run
A joy for all to see

How can we not see His light
When it shines before our eyes
How can we not feel the might
Of the love He does not hide

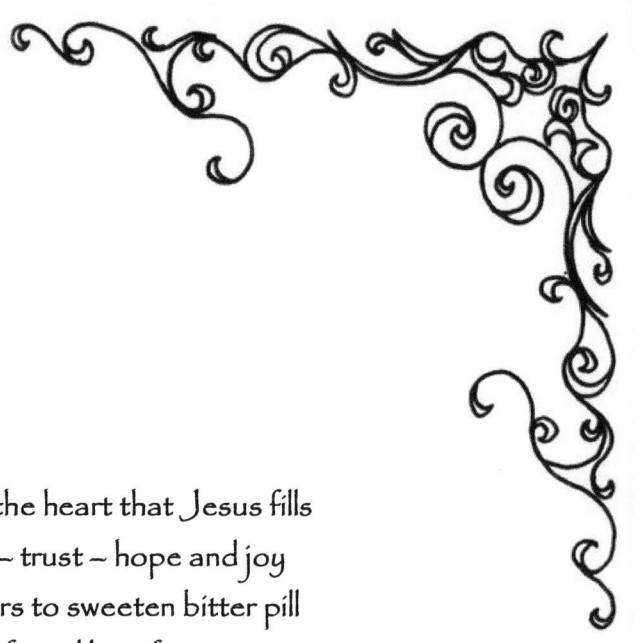

Love is the heart that Jesus fills
Faith – trust – hope and joy
Are ours to sweeten bitter pill
And comforts like a favourite toy

The love that does so gently touch
The troubles in our hearts
Will suddenly give so much
And troubles will soon depart

For love gives birth to grace
And grace comes to save
A gift that God gives us to taste
The joy of conquered grave

Your Voice

I rest, my Lord, upon Your word
I know that Yours is the voice I heard
For would the Spirit make sin to part
If not Your voice touched my heart

Your voice, my Lord, is a sound I see
For it changed all earthly things in me
It opened wide that closed tight door
You put goodness into my rotten core

When I looked through the open door
I saw rebirth, a life restored
Your Son had come to take me through
To the life where everything is new

I saw the truth of a wooden cross
Where Jesus had taken the sins I lost
His tortured body, a sacrifice
To heal my soul for His new life

For through the eyes of simple man
We will see the realm of the great "I AM"
The cross gave death to all our sins
That we may rise again to dwell with Him

Jesus Christ, God's own Son
Rose from the grave, the battle won
For in His hands he holds the power
To lift us up at the closing hour

The Golden Pathway

Our heart is a gateway to our soul
Whose keeper is the Holy Spirit
He warms our hearts from the evil cold
And lifts us high in the stirrup.

He is within us, the Holy One
Take heed to hear His call
He is the Spirit of Father and Son
And the love that has no wall.

There is no greater joy or font
Than to open our hearts to Him
And let Him know that all we want
Is to let His Spirit in.

The Light

There is a light beyond the sky
That gives the sky its light
And that same light is in our hearts
When we know the Lord Jesus Christ

The light that puts the devil to flight
The light that shows the way
The light that ends the darkest night
The light that brings the glorious day

The light that is Christ our Lord
The light that calms the soul
The light that melts the devils horde
The light that is God's precious gold

The Voice

There is a voice beyond our voice
That is so clear and true
It comes to us from heaven above
From Him that died for you

That voice is what we need to hear
Our daily bread He brings
And cast upon our troubles and fear
A light to devour our sins

And as the essence of that sound
Soaks into our heart and soul
It brings joy beyond all bounds
As Jesus comes to pay our toll

Love for the Lord

I know, oh Lord, that You are true
You lift me up in all I do
As a servant I follow You
And do the things You want me to

Lord, my prayer to You this day
Is to lift my heart that I may say
Thank you, Lord, for what is to come
And for Your blessings that have been done

Gracious Father, You are so good
You feed my heart with brotherhood
I want to do the things You do
And walk Your path that is straight and true

So, loving Father of love divine
Your love is like a shining shrine
That fills the hearts of all mankind
Till Your heaven we thankfully find

And now, my Lord, your love I taste
It's strengthens my legs to run the race
And as the race comes to a close
With You I win, I cannot lose

My love for You is like a fire
It's smallest flame has greatest power
It spreads so fast with burning desire
And reaches above the highest tower

My praise for You is forever more
It draws me through the open door
And there await the goals I need
The way, the truth and Your hand to lead

The Way

We do not know this coming day
What it holds within its sleeve
We know not the direction or the way
Or the power within the breeze

We know not how the sun will shine
Or where it's beams may fall
Or whether, like the finest wine
It's gone when we drink it all

We only know what ever part
Is played upon this day
That if God's love is in our heart
Then we will know the way

Jesus

When I wake and see the glorious day
May it be through the eyes of Jesus
When I see my neighbour
And they need God's love
May it be through the heart of Jesus
When I feel the joy within my heart
And I know the love that God imparts
May it be through the love of Jesus
When my time here is done at last
And through the veil I reach to grasp
May it be in the hands of Jesus

True Love

Lord, there is no weakness where love is true
There is no weakness in our love for You
You are the author of true love
You seal it by blessings from above

Lord, every day You hear our prayers
They can only be heard by You who cares
Our hearts will know what love can do
Our souls rejoice in the love from You

The sacrifice You made for us
Upon that cross you suffered thus
Your great love bore all our sins
Upon the cross where life begins

I see now beyond the sacrificial tree
The wondrous life You prepared for me
I see the path Your love has made
By Your precious love all my sins decay

Satan came one troubled day
He came to steal that love way
But he could not pass that wondrous cross
Where love was found and sin was lost

Gracious Lord, Your simple true love
Was blessed by our Father on the
wings of a dove
And that true love is ours to find
If we journey by the cross and
leave our sins behind

Loving Jesus, our Saviour dear
Your love for us is beyond compare
So help us Lord to know true love
That we may open heavens doors above

His Love

The beauty of the rising sun
That fills the morning sky
Is likened to the glorious love
That our Lord will never hide

But if we seek we shall find
And see Your wondrous face
Then heaven will show the final sign
And we will know – this is the place

For where you are Lord Jesus Christ
I want to dwell there too
To be at peace with all mankind
Your works and will to do

Into His Hands

In my thoughts, my mind I unfold
In my sight, a palace I behold
A place of gold like a fortress stands
A place that nestles in God's own hands.

Its gates were opened as I drew near
I see this place in my daily prayer
There were no words upon the door
But through its portals, heaven I saw.

As I searched for the true path in
I saw hurrying people filled with sin
They walked right past the open door
They could not see, their sight was poor.

I slowed my pace, to halt my haste
I needed time to pray, and God's water to taste
For when I enter those gates of gold
My soul will be ready for what I behold.

The unrighteous path is large and clear
The ungodly follow it and have no fear
That path will come to where Satan's fire burns
A path to hell that has no return.

I love my Lord with all my heart
I find heaven's path where sins depart
God's love has conquered the evil hate
And His Son, my Jesus, is at heaven's gate.

He stands there at the open door
I see angels around those portals, soar
Jesus is there, arms open wide
He still has the scars on wrists and side.

I know then, this is my goal
I know the path, I am no fool
Heaven beamed suddenly from earthly gloom
At last, with Jesus, I am home.

Cleansing Waters

So bright the light that comes to me
When I hear the voice of God
Precious gifts for all to see
When we walk where Jesus trod

Behind me are the gates of hell
Ahead God's heaven is calling
Keep onward where you will find the well
Of the Living Water that is cleansing

Coming Home

Lord help me to follow You by Your light
Help me to keep You in my sight
Help me by Your hand of might
That we at last may win the fight

You stand by the portals of heaven's gate
And you see us coming, we won't be late
Our stride is lengthening as we draw near
As heavenly songs of joy we hear

And then we see our journey's end
We have just come round the final bend
And then we gasp with wonder and awe
And we see You waiting at the door

Lord Jesus You greet us with open arms
And we are calmed by Your glorious charm
You push those gates open wide
And there reveal Your realm inside

COME LORD JESUS

From Death to Glory

The holiness of Your sanctuary, Lord
Was too much for my weak mind
So I took another path, my Lord
A path of fear and grime

The fields I ploughed had turned sour
The fruits no longer could I devour
For the darkness over my soul that came
Was evil, desolation and punishing pain

But then through the wonder of God's grace
He took the bitter and gave sweet taste
And by the greatness of His love
I found again my Lord above

Come

As the world grows dark in Satan's grasp
The time has come, oh Lord, at last
For Your church to leave at Your command
Your mighty voice and the sudden calm
When we will come unto our King
And to His home our soul He brings
Lord and Saviour of mankind
We hear Your voice, that voice is divine
And we come to You, the battle done
The evil gone and victory won

Wondrous Heaven

Help us Lord to see the way
The footsteps you have trod
And Lord we seek that coming day
When You take us home to God

The heaven that is beyond compare
Will fill our wildest dreams
Beyond all that nature wears
Living waters and eternal streams

If our eyes are on our Lord
And we follow his footsteps true
Then we will pass that final veil
And His hand will wait for you

The Coming Hour

Lord, help me foil the tempter's power
And save my soul before final hour
The blessed hope is coming near
I must be worthy – when Your voice I hear

If my distress clutters the path
Then sweep it clean, and let me pass
And as I approach this life's end
You will say, "Come, good and faithful friend"

So by your grace my life is led
And by Your word, this body fed
And by Your love that dwells in me
Your blood has cleansed and set me free

Heavenly Father, hear my prayer
And take me to that final stair
The step that takes me through the veil
To take that hand, pierced by the nail

As final verse of scripture say
The last prayer before final day
To you, our Lord, our Father's Son
It reads, "COME, LORD JESUS, COME"

AMEN

The day God called you Home

God looked around his garden
And found an empty place
He then looked down upon the earth
And saw your tired face
He put His arms around you
And lifted you to rest
God's garden must be beautiful
He always takes the best

He saw your road was getting rough
And the hills were hard to climb
So He closed your weary eyes
And whispered 'peace be thine'
It broke our hearts to lose you
But you didn't go alone
For part of us went with you
The day God called you home

He knew that you were suffering
He knew you were in pain
And He knew that you would never
Get well on earth again
It broke our hearts to lose you
But you didn't go alone
For the Lord, he went with you
The day He called you home

You left us precious memories
Your love will be our guide
Your strength always inspired us
Until the day you died
It broke our hearts to lose you
But you didn't go alone
For part of us went with you
The day God called you home

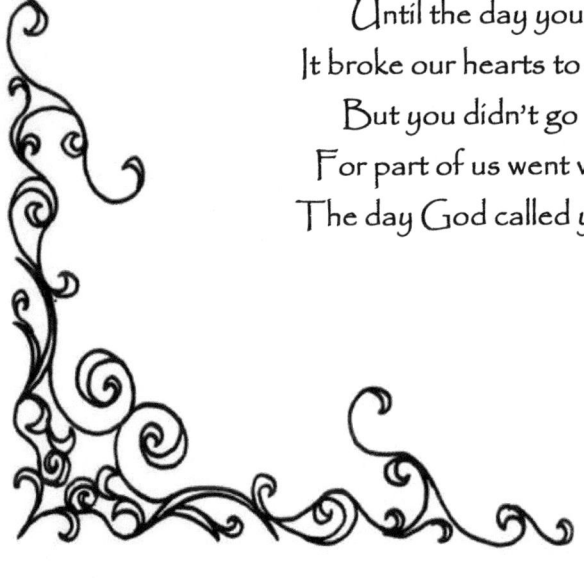

The Great Divide

When I cross that great divide
When I enter the body that You provide
Lord Jesus, may I hold Your hand
That you may take me to Your promised land

My spirit is filled with love You gave
The love that entered my life to save
To save me from that fiery glow
Of the burning death with Satan below

What joy You gave my heart that day
When You opened my eyes and taught me to pray
In prayer I found that secret door
The door that was a secret no more

It was no vision before my eyes
When You said to me "my son arise
And see new life I give to you
That you be as clean as the morning dew"

"I see no past sin if you walk with Me
If you accept My truth which will set you free
Free from the shackles of sin and shame
To a life where truth is the name of the game"

"This life I give you is filled with love
The greatest love from God above
I tell you now, hear my last law
Love one another in the truth I bore"

Homeward Bound

Lord, You are the light that leadeth me
You are the light that set me free
You are the light that fills my room
You are the light that takes me home

Lord, may Your light shine on me
And fill my eyes that I may see
Fill my heart and make it whole
Fill the gap that Satan stole

Refresh my life by Your gentle hand
That I may see Your promised land
Now my soul has found it's home
Take it my Lord, never more to roam

Wondrous, gentle Lamb of God
May I walk with You and hold Your rod
Open the gate and let me in
Forgiven, my Lord, of my past sin

Days grow short, this life grows dim
Let Your light soothe my aching limbs
I've passed not into darkened night
I come to You, Lord, Your light shines ever bright

Beware

I know that in the coming hours
That Satan will exert his powers
A storm will strike my body and soul
And cast his lies to build a mould

But I will call upon the Lord
And he will give me a worthy sword
And when I swing that sword so true
Satan will flee and the storm subdue

So great the powers of Christ our Lord
That evil becomes a broken cord
When from the tongue of the risen Christ
Demands – be gone from this precious life

Your Light

Lord Jesus, take me to Your light
Protect me from the devil's fight
Be my guide through darkest storm
So I may see the heavenly morn

This earth and all around me wane
And I will lose the earthly pain
Then my spirit will rejoice
When I hear Your heavenly voice

So angels play your harps aloud
Let singing come from every cloud
At last my Lord has come to say
Welcome home you are here to stay

The Fallen

The night is dark, all is silent
The heat of battle has burned it's wrath
Those that paid the price of war so violent
Lay in the dust that is now past

In the fields of battle, suffering and strife
Comes the prayer to save them, from mother and wife
For in the battle many will fall
And we pray, dear Lord, you hear their call

On foreign land, in alien soil
Rest the fallen who have given their all
And we that are favoured by what they have given
Give thanks to God for their deeds and heroism

In the fields of battle where poppies grow
Lay sons and fathers from family home
Sacrificial seed was sown here
And the voice of prayer defeated the doom

In the fields where the fallen lay
Comes the voice of one that earnestly pray
God, take my soul, for death is near
And lift me up from the evil here

We pray for the fallen in lands at war
That your spirit may touch them so they cry no more
That they may come where hate has ceased
Into the arms of Jesus, the Prince of Peace

Thank you for Your trusted hand
That has taken us through the night
And delivered us to Your heavenly land
To bathe in Your heavenly light

So, Lord, on this Remembrance Day
We turn our thoughts from work and play
And remember those that in battle fell
And thank You for the peace in which we now dwell

Shelter from the Storm

The Almighty wings of the Lord our God
Spread over all the earth
And those who accept His loving word
Are sheltered beneath their girth

And in the shelter of His wings
We dwell where we can shout
Our praises to our Lord and King
And keep all evil out

Open your hearts, you people of God
And let our Saviour in
For He will trample the very sod
That harbours all our sin

Know what our Saviour said
I am the beginning and the end
So when we pray and our scripture read
Praise Him first – for He is the end

Awake

I hear the voice of morning call
And feel the realm of sleep depart
And waiting on the wings of dawn
Is Jesus to rekindle my heart

He has watched my voyage through the night
And any bad dreams He put to flight
I see him in my vision clear
He drives away any doubt or fear

He then takes me by the hand
To guide me through my daily span
With Him I avoid all ills and woe
And shake the hand of all my foe

A loving God is ours to see
If we take the hand that is offered free
Put our love and trust in his care
And see His Kingdom as it draws near

Tribulation

In the fiercest storm and great unrest
When thunder rocks the heavens
The earth will move from beneath our feet
Throwing fire from boiling caverns

We will know how God's hand is here
And His voice becomes a whisper
If we fall upon our knees
And burst that evil blister

He is forgiving, our loving God
And He loves his children dear
If we would live by His word
Then sin becomes a fear

Printed in Great Britain
by Amazon